POPE
FRANCIS

BY EMANUEL CASTRO   ILLUSTRATED BY IGNACIO SEGESSO

CAPSTONE PRESS
a capstone imprint

Graphic Library is published by Capstone Press,
1710 Roe Crest Drive, North Mankato, Minnesota 56003
www.mycapstone.com

Cataloging-in-Publication Data is available on the Library
of Congress website.
ISBN 978-1-5157-9162-1 (library binding)
ISBN 978-1-5157-9166-9 (paperback)
ISBN 978-1-5157-9170-6 (paperback)

Summary: Follow the extraordinary life of Pope Francis in
this unofficial biography.

Author: Emanuel Castro
Illustrator: Ignacio Segesso

Translated into the English language by
Trusted Translations

Printed in the United States of America.
010370F17

TABLE OF CONTENTS

CHAPTER 1
A SIMPLE CHILDHOOD

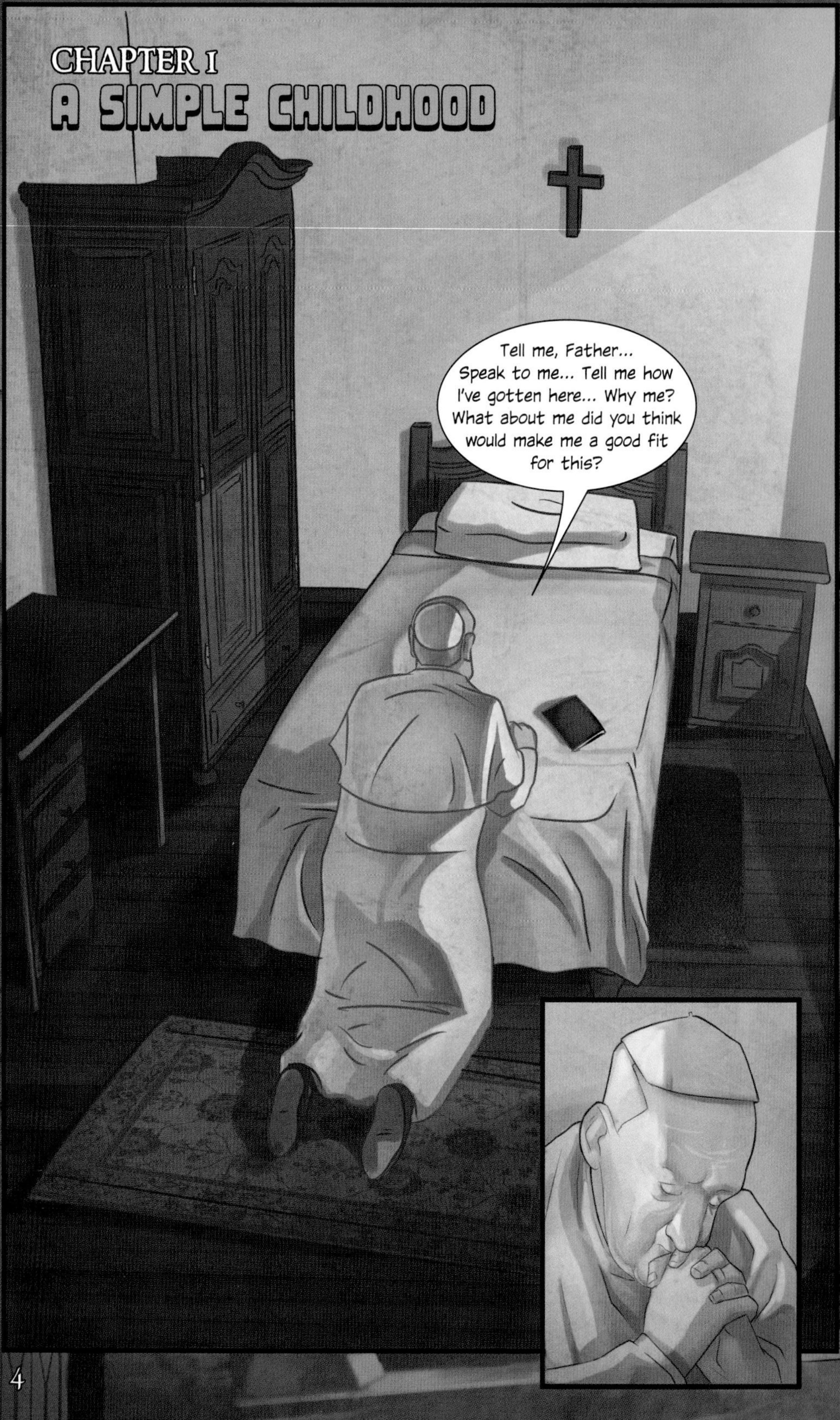
Tell me, Father... Speak to me... Tell me how I've gotten here... Why me? What about me did you think would make me a good fit for this?

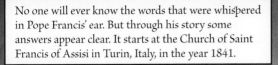

No one will ever know the words that were whispered in Pope Francis' ear. But through his story some answers appear clear. It starts at the Church of Saint Francis of Assisi in Turin, Italy, in the year 1841.

This is unthinkable in this church! When you are ordered to pray, pray; when you are ordered to confess, confess!

Ah, Father! You're hurting me! Ouch!

It's ok, Father. I'll take care of him.

Why was the sexton yelling at you, boy?

Because I don't know how to be an acolyte.

Tell me, have you taken communion?

No, Father. I don't know the catechism, either. I'm poor. My parents left me.

5

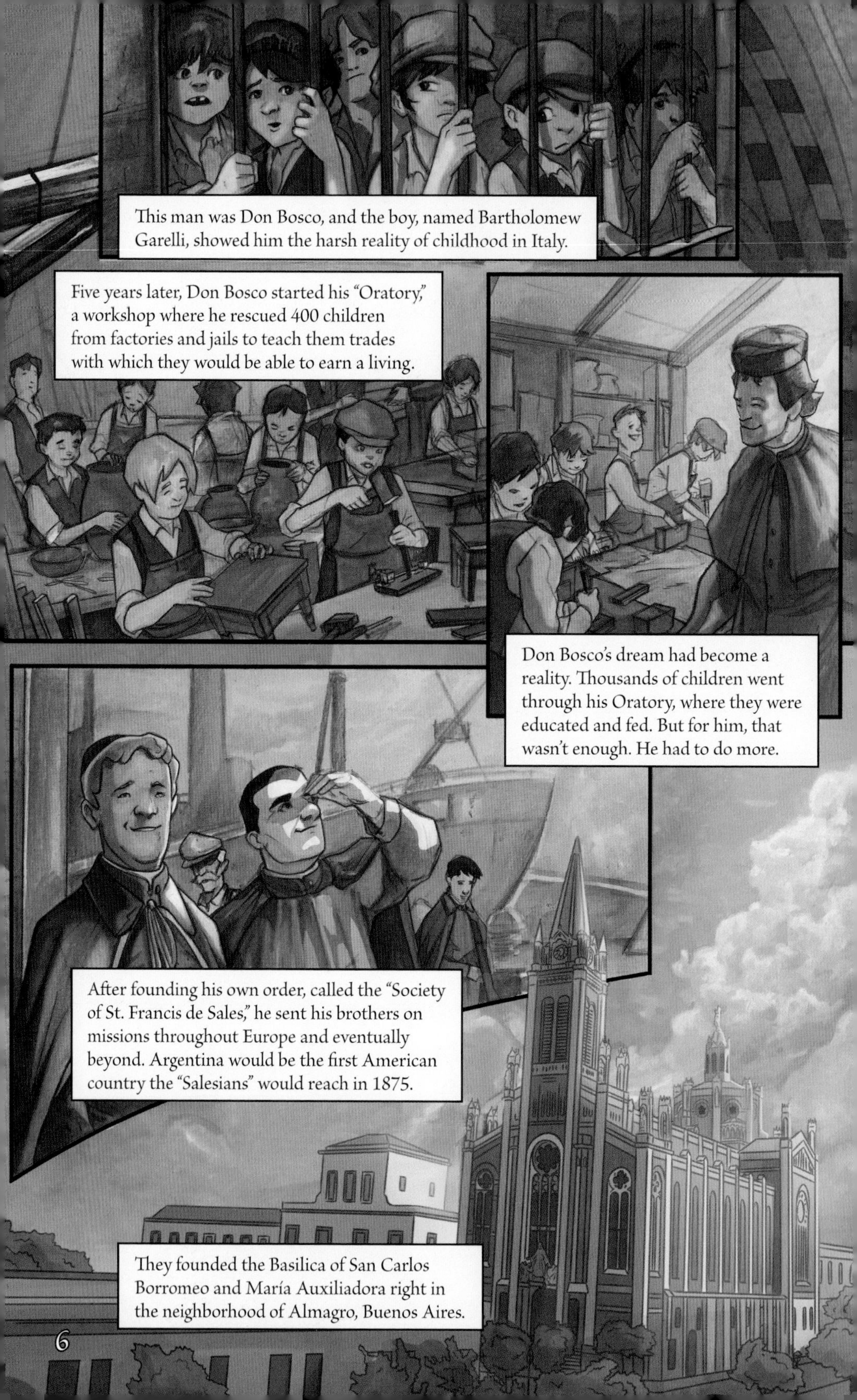
This man was Don Bosco, and the boy, named Bartholomew Garelli, showed him the harsh reality of childhood in Italy.
Five years later, Don Bosco started his "Oratory," a workshop where he rescued 400 children from factories and jails to teach them trades with which they would be able to earn a living.
Don Bosco's dream had become a reality. Thousands of children went through his Oratory, where they were educated and fed. But for him, that wasn't enough. He had to do more.
After founding his own order, called the "Society of St. Francis de Sales," he sent his brothers on missions throughout Europe and eventually beyond. Argentina would be the first American country the "Salesians" would reach in 1875.
They founded the Basilica of San Carlos Borromeo and María Auxiliadora right in the neighborhood of Almagro, Buenos Aires.

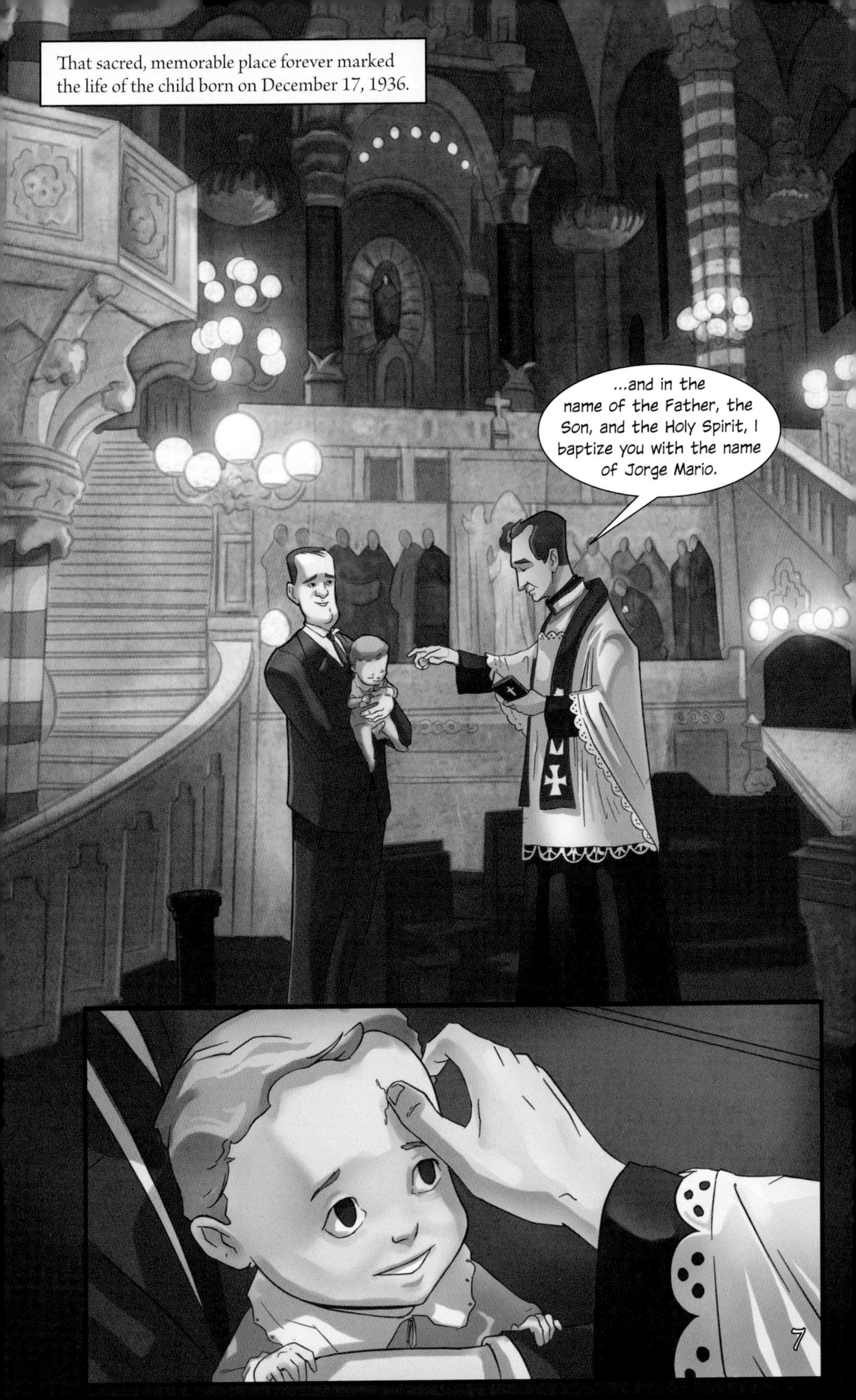
That sacred, memorable place forever marked the life of the child born on December 17, 1936.
...and in the name of the Father, the Son, and the Holy Spirit, I baptize you with the name of Jorge Mario.

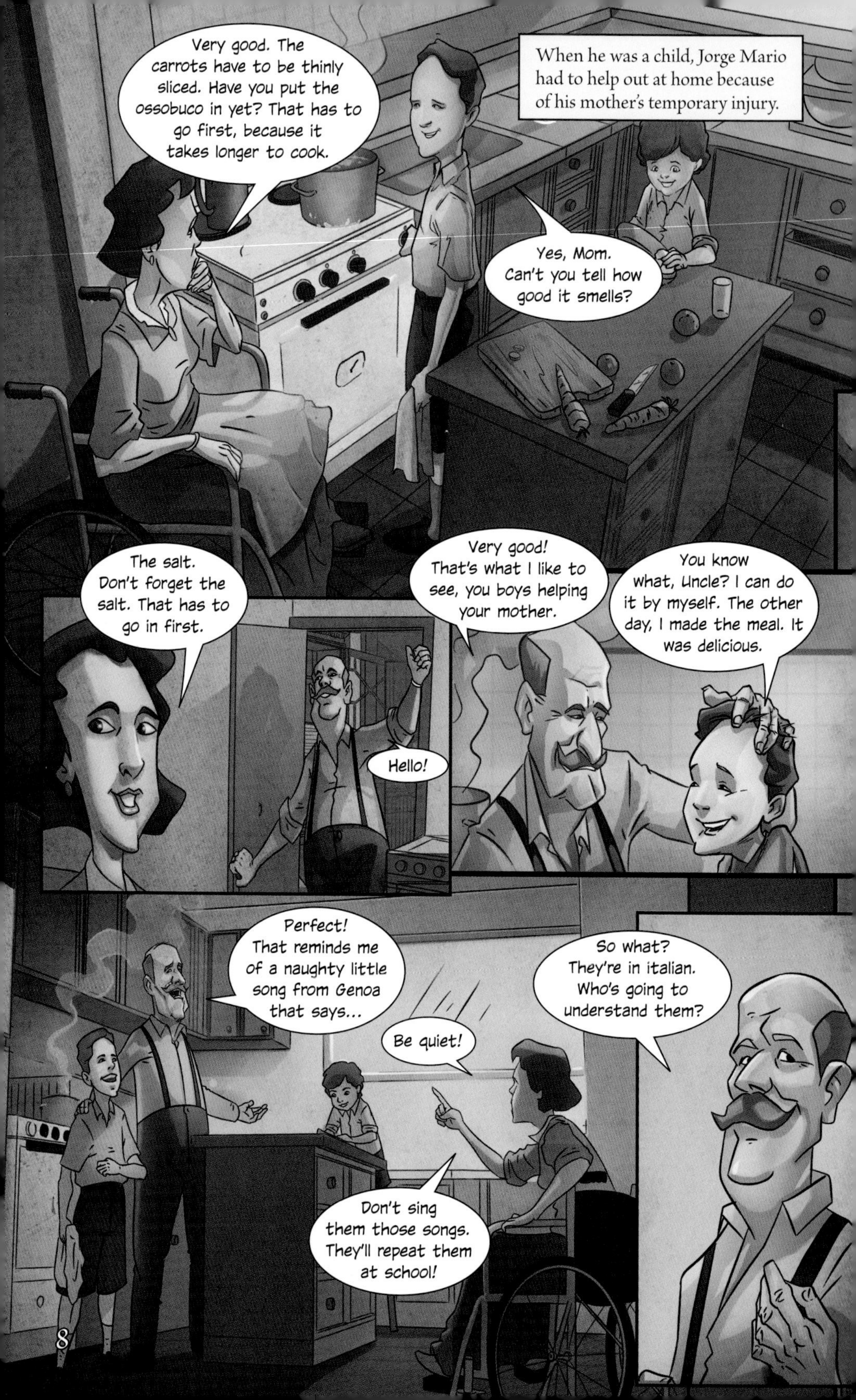

When he was a child, Jorge Mario had to help out at home because of his mother's temporary injury.
Very good. The carrots have to be thinly sliced. Have you put the ossobuco in yet? That has to go first, because it takes longer to cook.
Yes, Mom. Can't you tell how good it smells?
The salt. Don't forget the salt. That has to go in first.
Hello!
Very good! That's what I like to see, you boys helping your mother.
You know what, Uncle? I can do it by myself. The other day, I made the meal. It was delicious.
Perfect! That reminds me of a naughty little song from Genoa that says...
Be quiet!
Don't sing them those songs. They'll repeat them at school!
So what? They're in italian. Who's going to understand them?

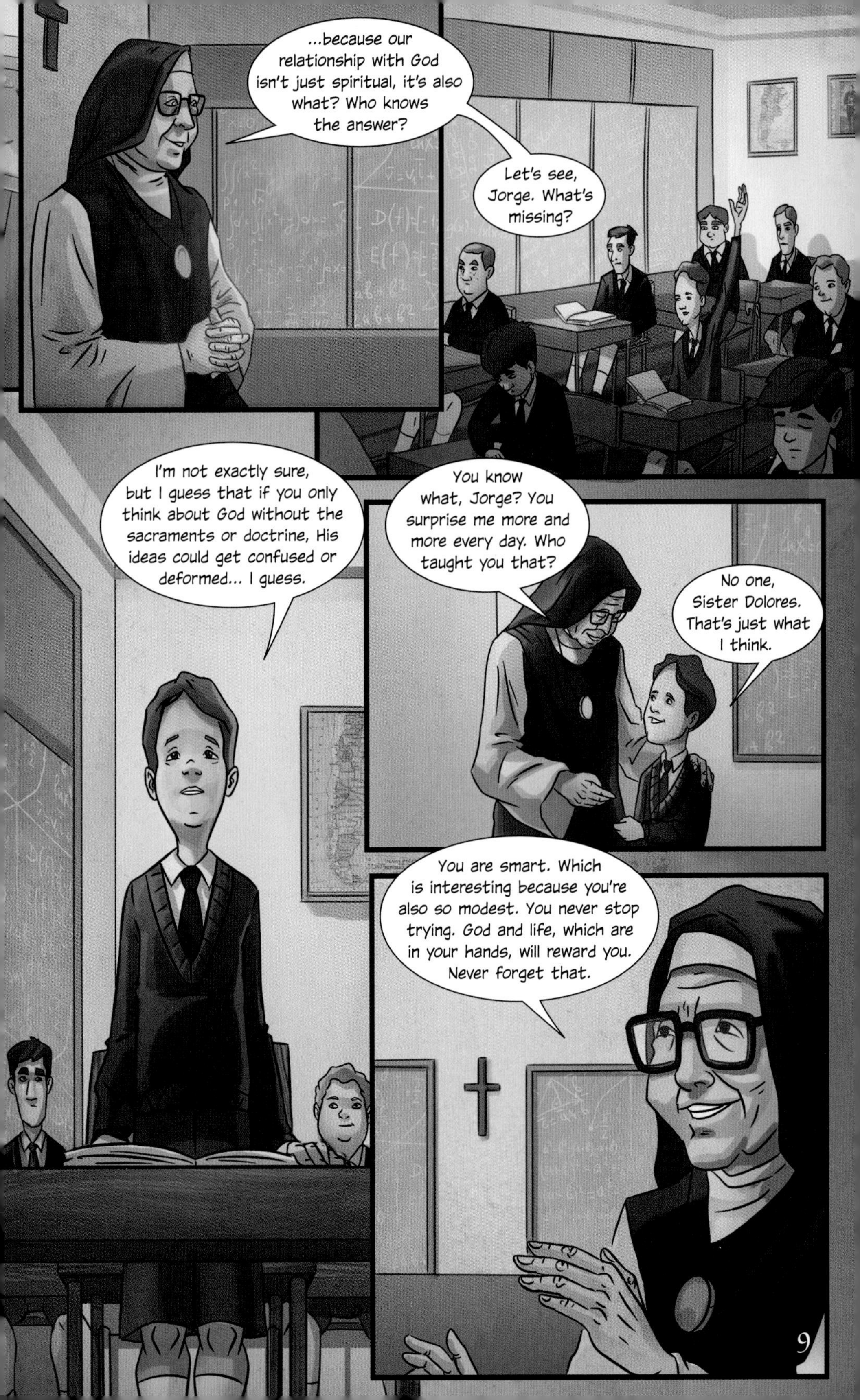

...because our relationship with God isn't just spiritual, it's also what? Who knows the answer?
Let's see, Jorge. What's missing?
I'm not exactly sure, but I guess that if you only think about God without the sacraments or doctrine, His ideas could get confused or deformed... I guess.
You know what, Jorge? You surprise me more and more every day. Who taught you that?
No one, Sister Dolores. That's just what I think.
You are smart. Which is interesting because you're also so modest. You never stop trying. God and life, which are in your hands, will reward you. Never forget that.

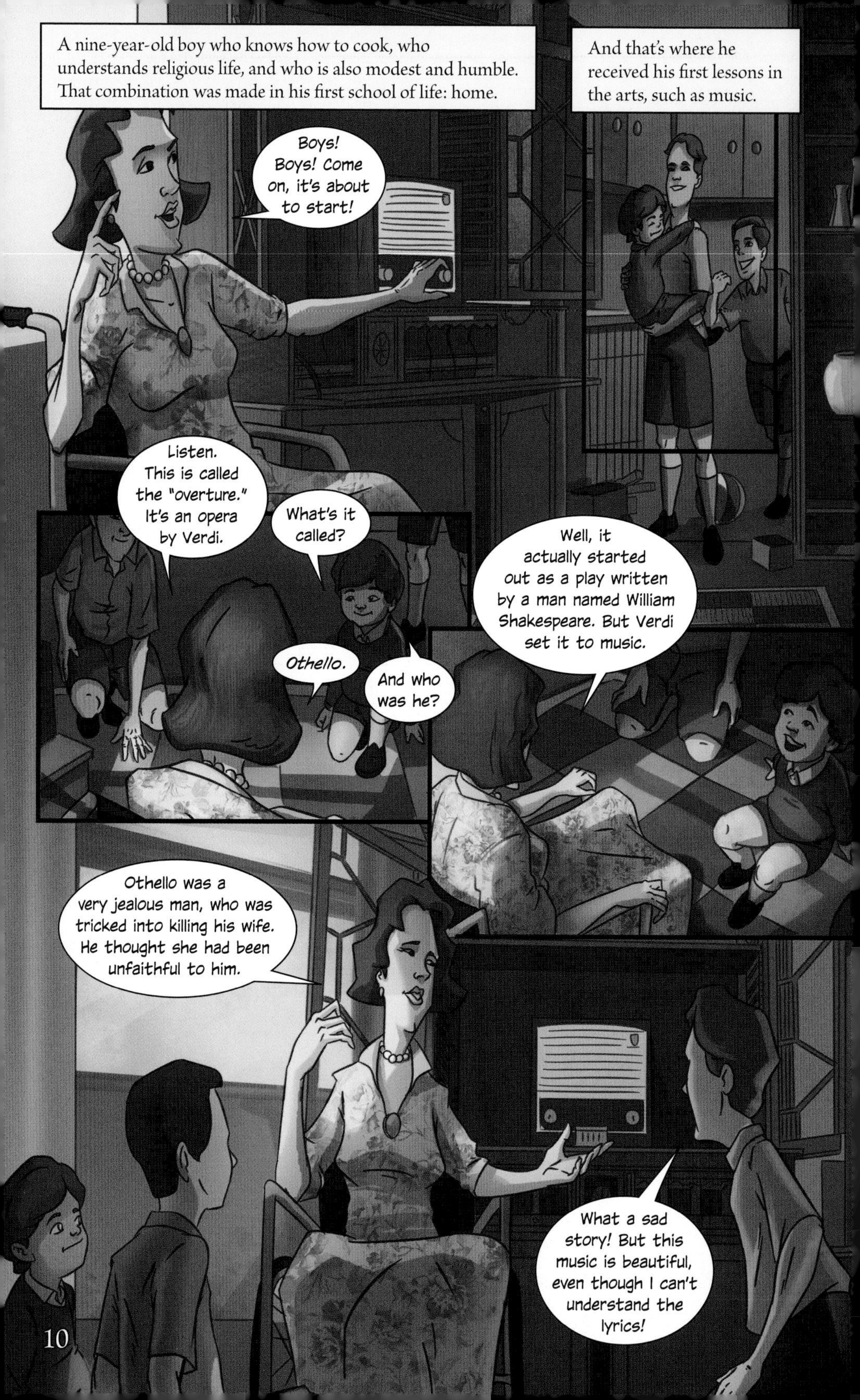
A nine-year-old boy who knows how to cook, who understands religious life, and who is also modest and humble. That combination was made in his first school of life: home.
And that's where he received his first lessons in the arts, such as music.
Boys! Boys! Come on, it's about to start!
Listen. This is called the "overture." It's an opera by Verdi.
What's it called?
Othello.
And who was he?
Well, it actually started out as a play written by a man named William Shakespeare. But Verdi set it to music.
Othello was a very jealous man, who was tricked into killing his wife. He thought she had been unfaithful to him.
What a sad story! But this music is beautiful, even though I can't understand the lyrics!

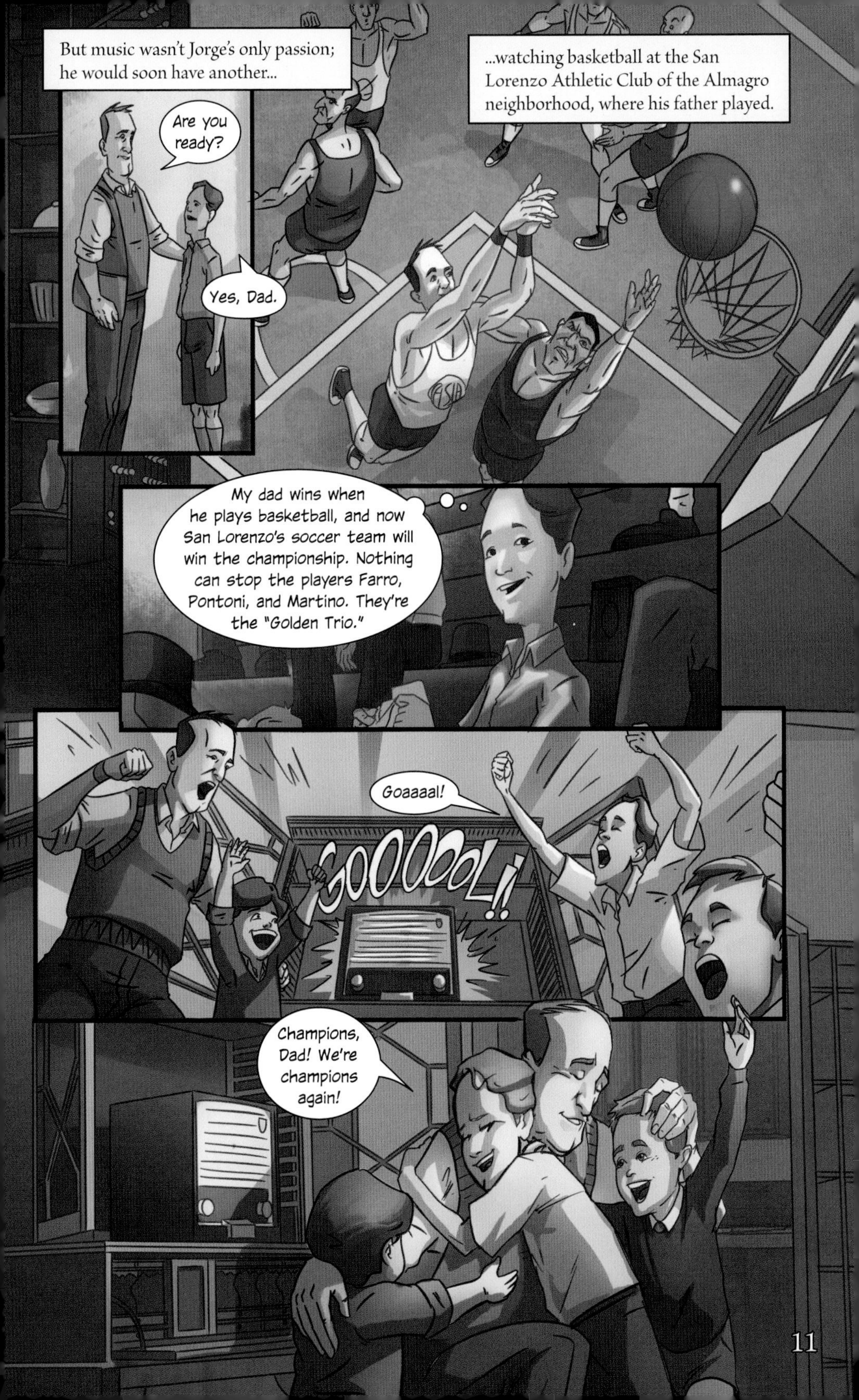

But music wasn't Jorge's only passion; he would soon have another...
Are you ready?
Yes, Dad.
...watching basketball at the San Lorenzo Athletic Club of the Almagro neighborhood, where his father played.
My dad wins when he plays basketball, and now San Lorenzo's soccer team will win the championship. Nothing can stop the players Farro, Pontoni, and Martino. They're the "Golden Trio."
Goaaaal!
GOOOOOL!!
Champions, Dad! We're champions again!

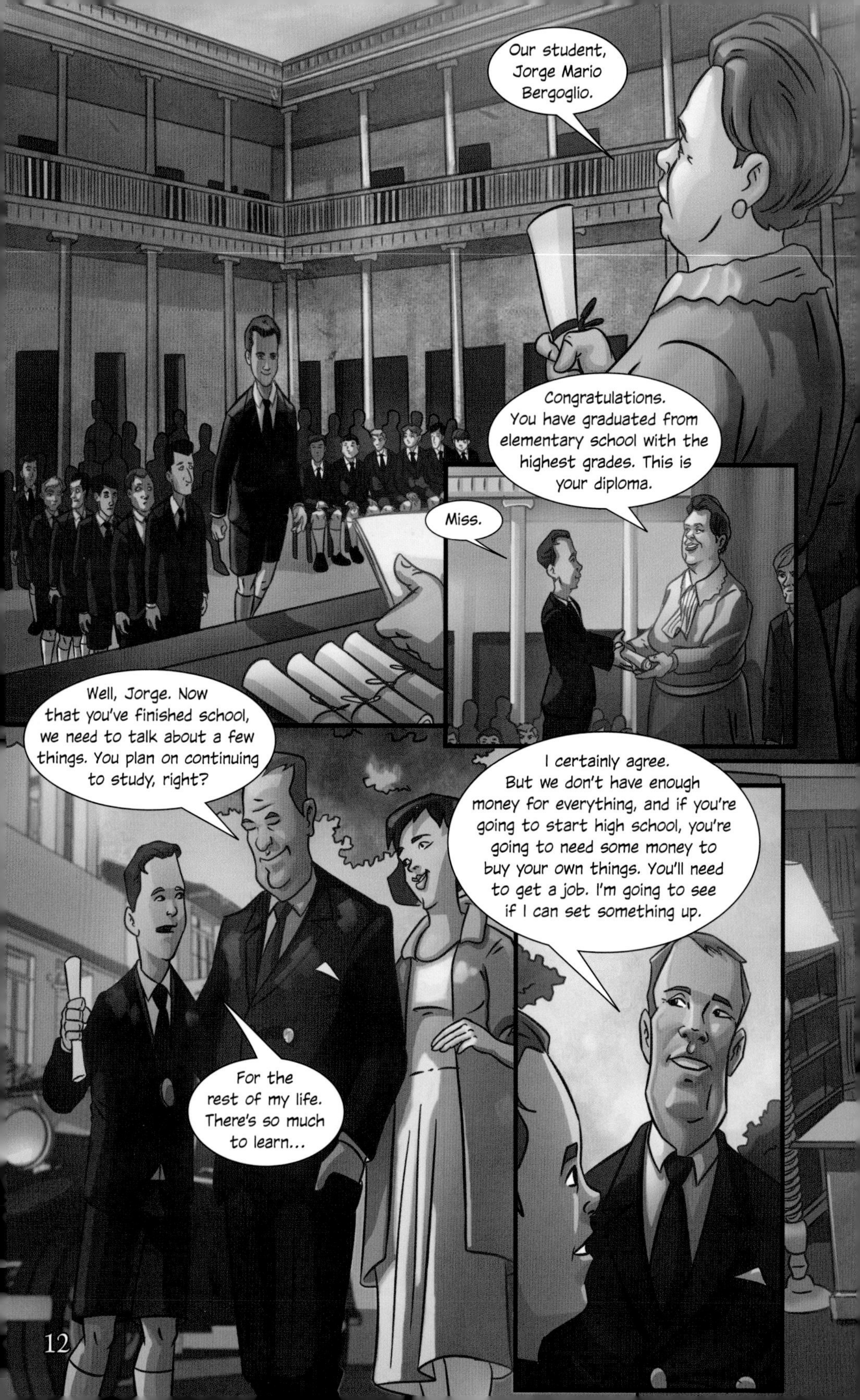
Our student, Jorge Mario Bergoglio.
Congratulations. You have graduated from elementary school with the highest grades. This is your diploma.
Miss.
Well, Jorge. Now that you've finished school, we need to talk about a few things. You plan on continuing to study, right?
For the rest of my life. There's so much to learn...
I certainly agree. But we don't have enough money for everything, and if you're going to start high school, you're going to need some money to buy your own things. You'll need to get a job. I'm going to see if I can set something up.

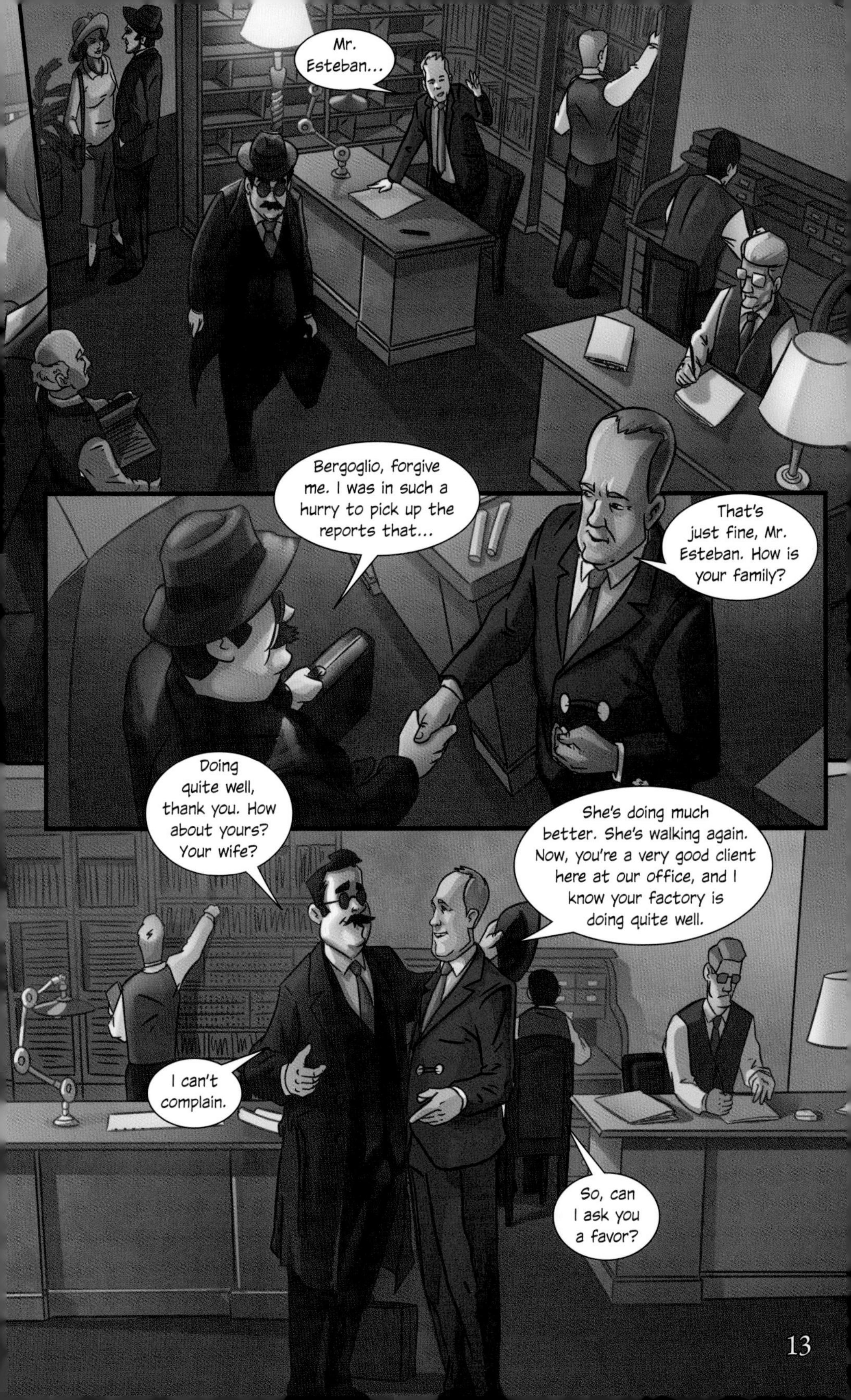
Mr. Esteban...
Bergoglio, forgive me. I was in such a hurry to pick up the reports that...
That's just fine, Mr. Esteban. How is your family?
Doing quite well, thank you. How about yours? Your wife?
She's doing much better. She's walking again. Now, you're a very good client here at our office, and I know your factory is doing quite well.
I can't complain.
So, can I ask you a favor?

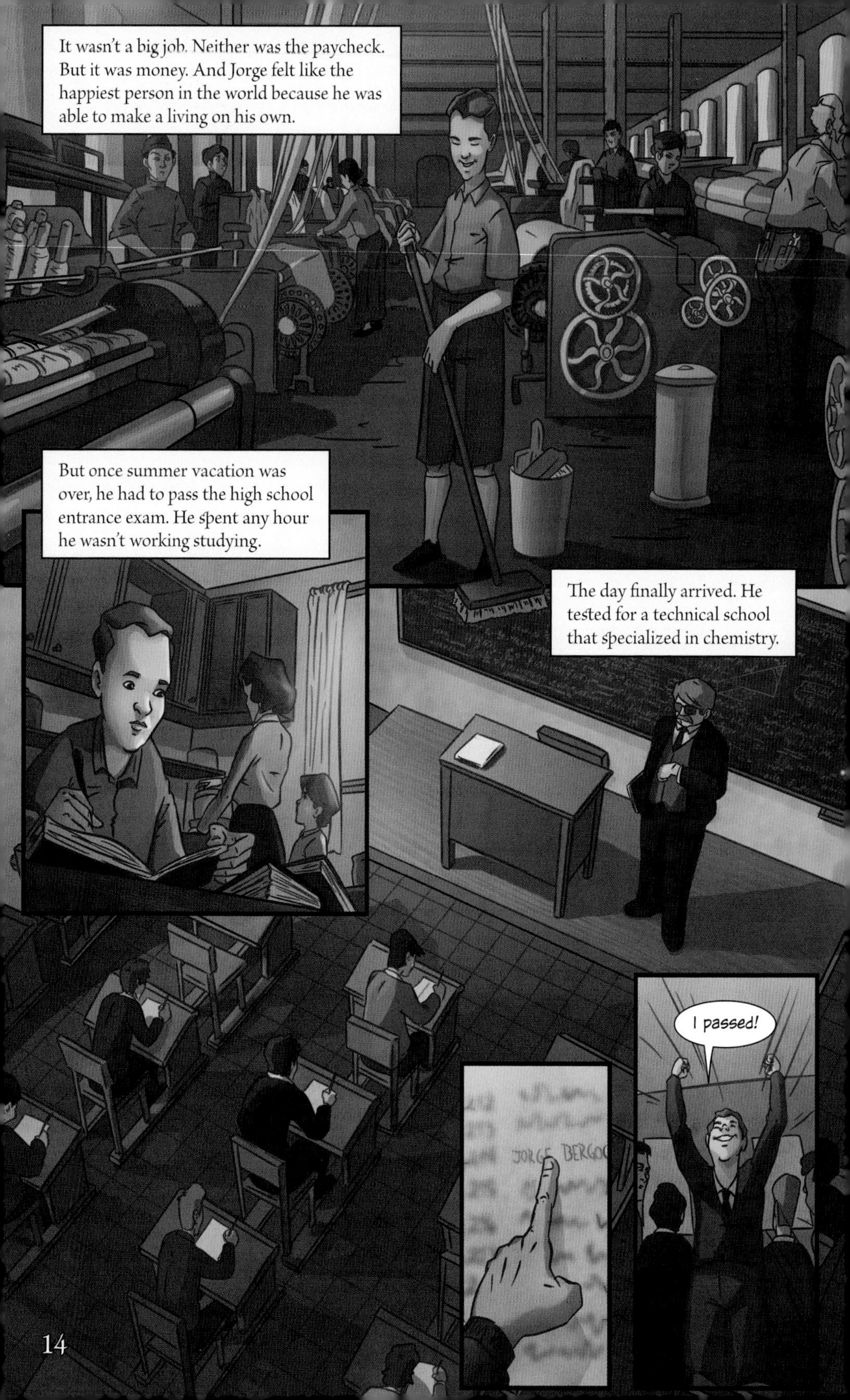
It wasn't a big job. Neither was the paycheck. But it was money. And Jorge felt like the happiest person in the world because he was able to make a living on his own.
But once summer vacation was over, he had to pass the high school entrance exam. He spent any hour he wasn't working studying.
The day finally arrived. He tested for a technical school that specialized in chemistry.
I passed!

Jorgito, can you come here for a second?
Your father is an excellent man, and you remind me of him. You're always on time, you never miss work, and you always have an answer for everything.
Since you're in high school now, and we need staff who know how to do calculations, I was wondering if you would like to work in administration. We would pay you more money.
Of course!

CHAPTER 2
BETWEEN LIFE AND DEATH

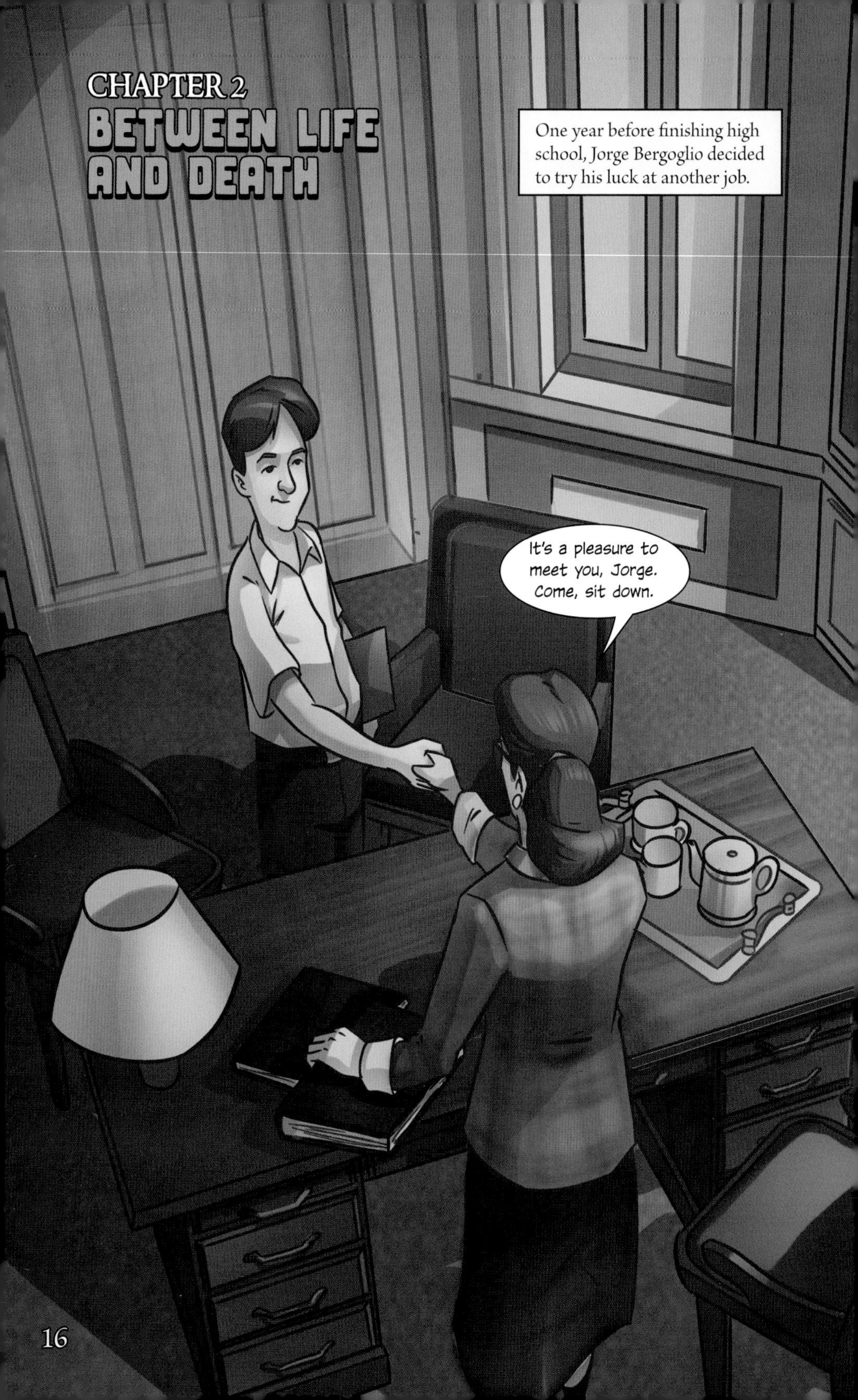
One year before finishing high school, Jorge Bergoglio decided to try his luck at another job.
It's a pleasure to meet you, Jorge. Come, sit down.

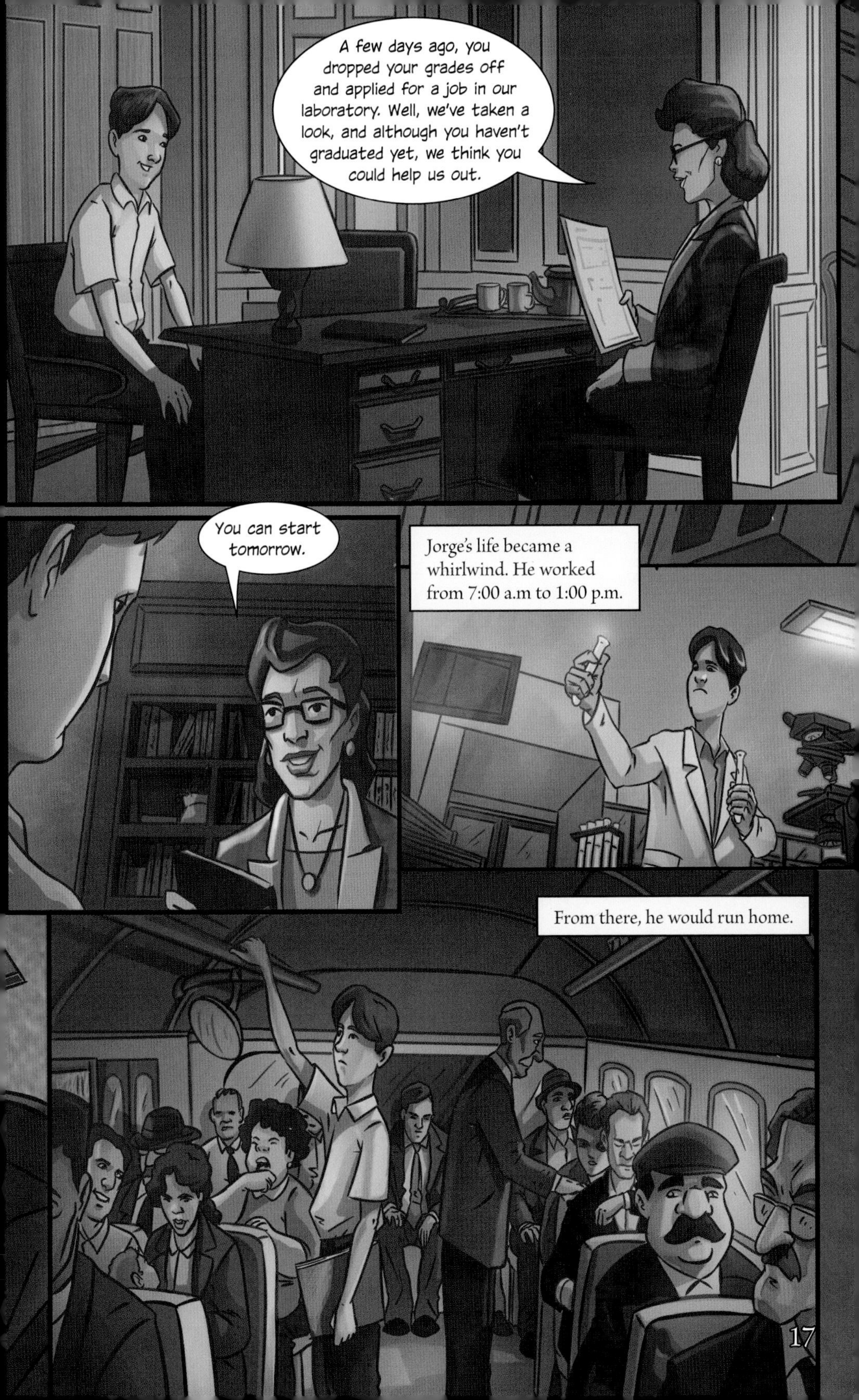
A few days ago, you dropped your grades off and applied for a job in our laboratory. Well, we've taken a look, and although you haven't graduated yet, we think you could help us out.
You can start tomorrow.
Jorge's life became a whirlwind. He worked from 7:00 a.m to 1:00 p.m.
From there, he would run home.

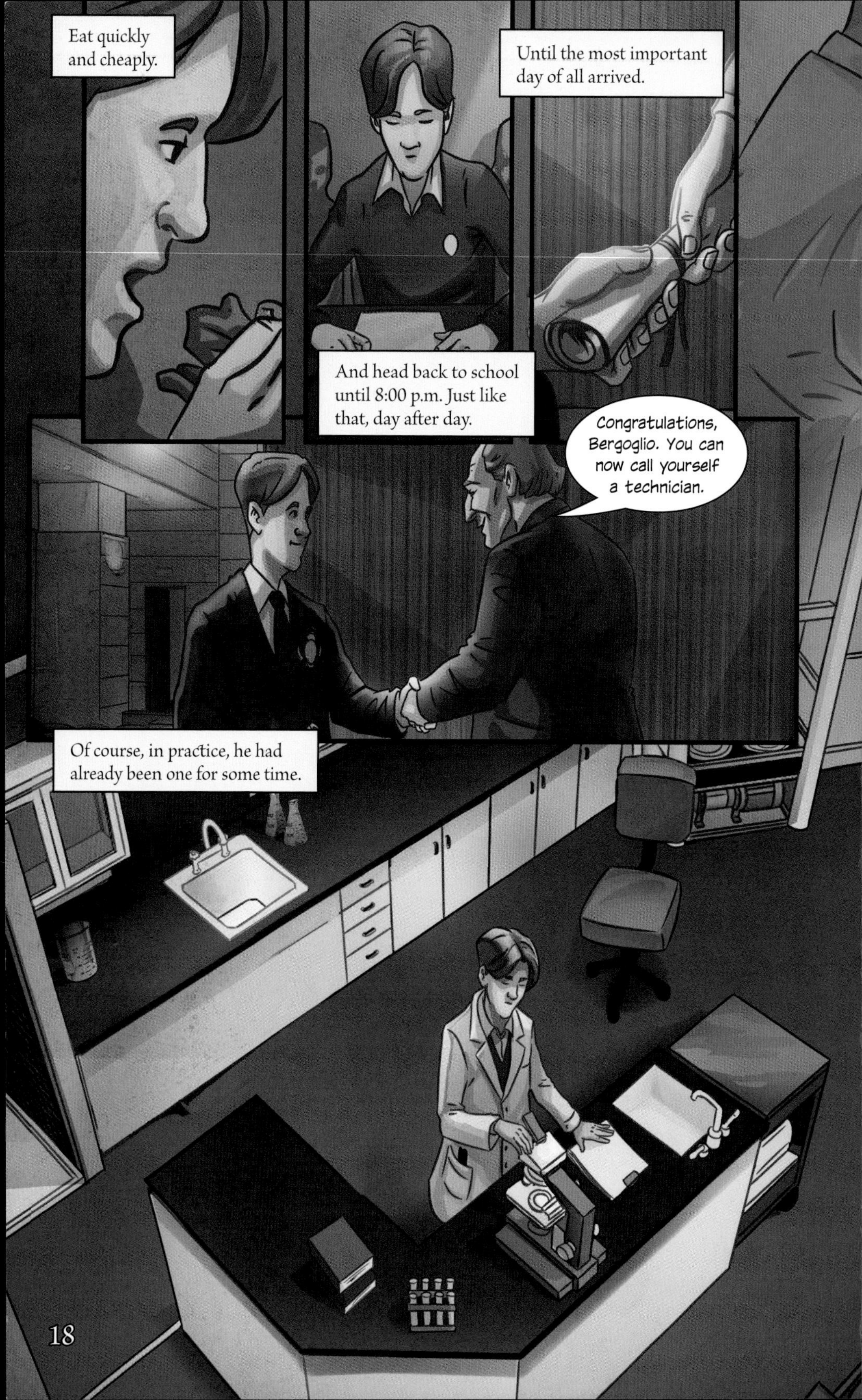
Eat quickly and cheaply.
And head back to school until 8:00 p.m. Just like that, day after day.
Until the most important day of all arrived.
Congratulations, Bergoglio. You can now call yourself a technician.
Of course, in practice, he had already been one for some time.

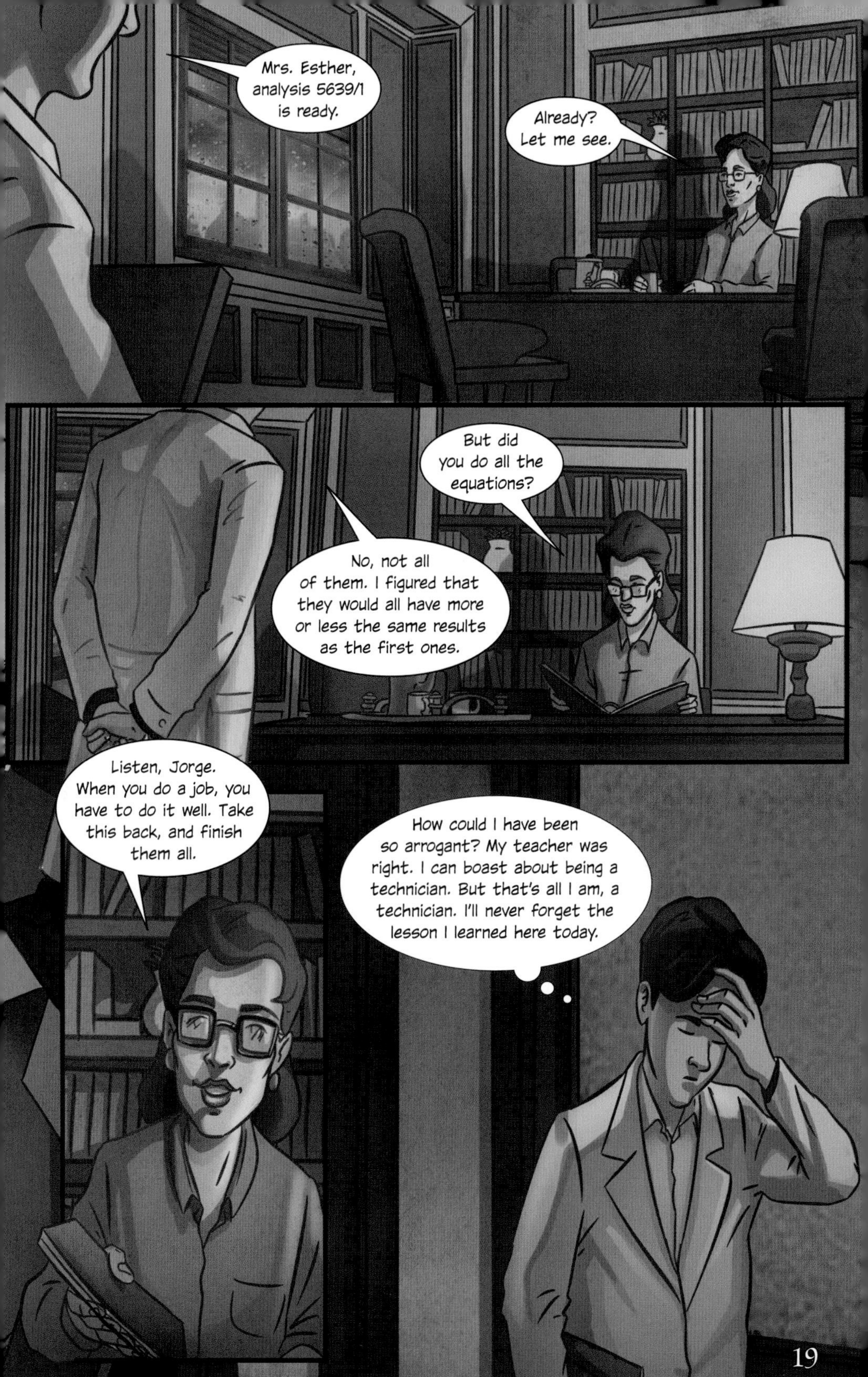
Mrs. Esther, analysis 5639/1 is ready.
Already? Let me see.
But did you do all the equations?
No, not all of them. I figured that they would all have more or less the same results as the first ones.
Listen, Jorge. When you do a job, you have to do it well. Take this back, and finish them all.
How could I have been so arrogant? My teacher was right. I can boast about being a technician. But that's all I am, a technician. I'll never forget the lesson I learned here today.

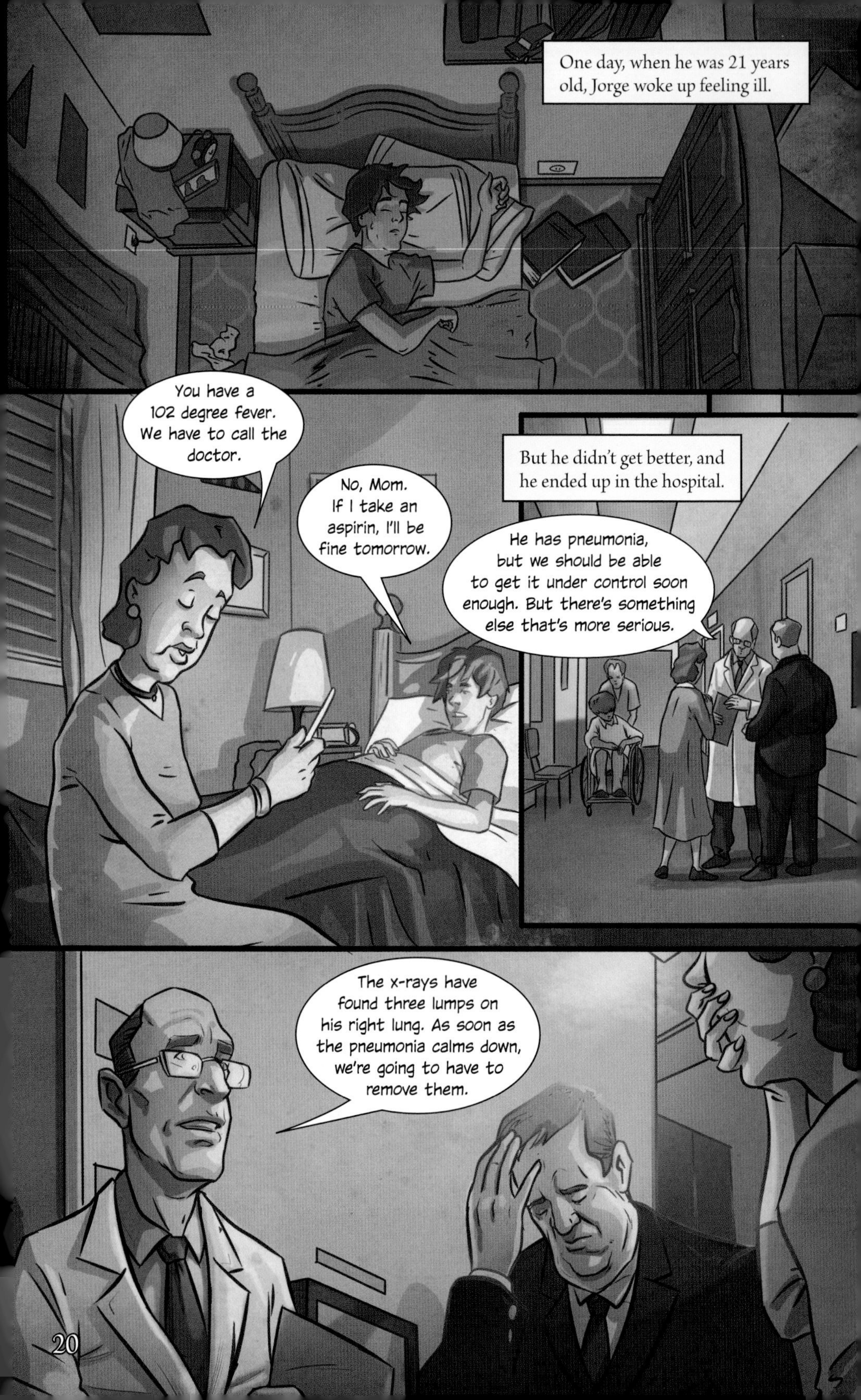
One day, when he was 21 years old, Jorge woke up feeling ill.
You have a 102 degree fever. We have to call the doctor.
No, Mom. If I take an aspirin, I'll be fine tomorrow.
But he didn't get better, and he ended up in the hospital.
He has pneumonia, but we should be able to get it under control soon enough. But there's something else that's more serious.
The x-rays have found three lumps on his right lung. As soon as the pneumonia calms down, we're going to have to remove them.

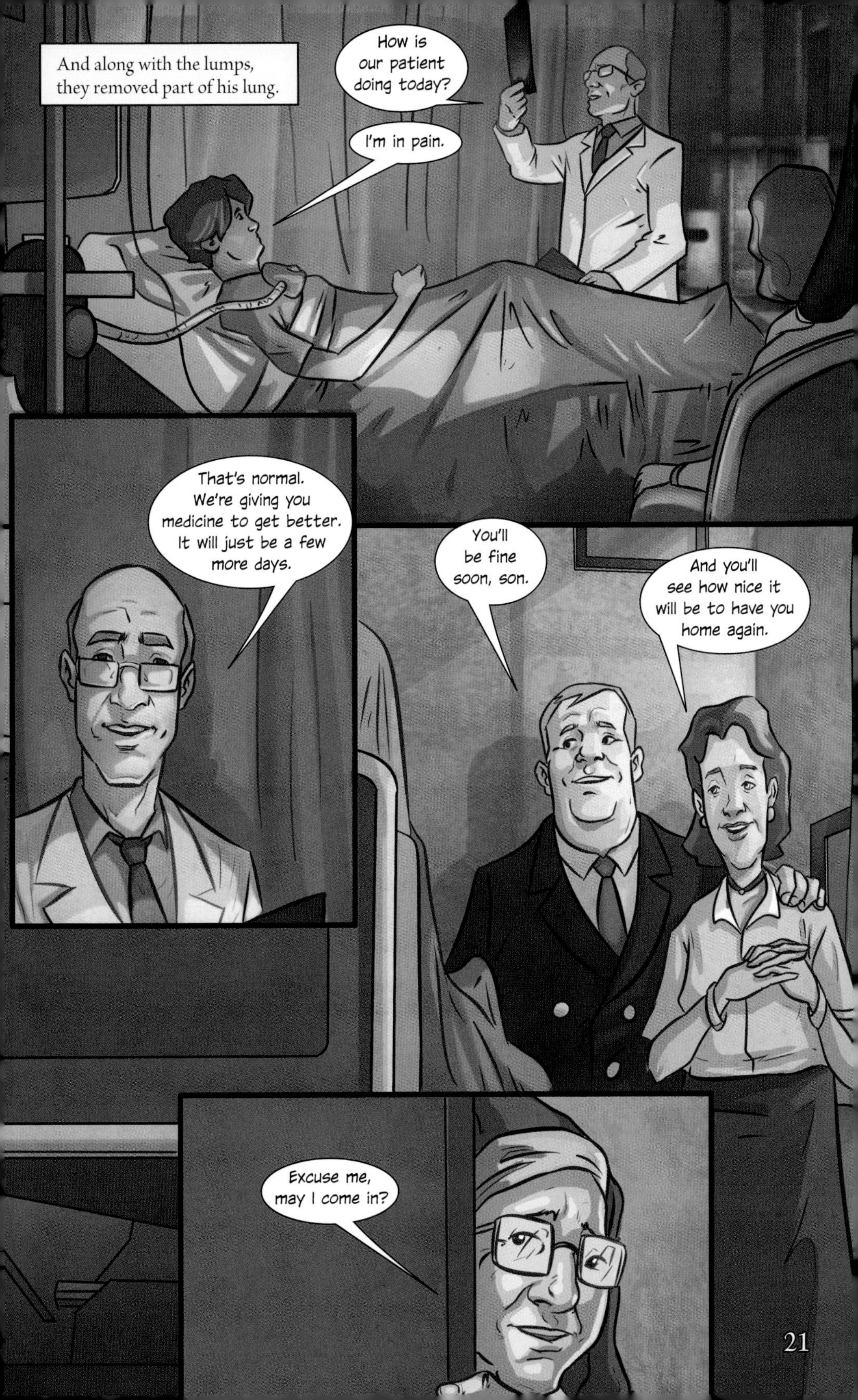
And along with the lumps, they removed part of his lung.
How is our patient doing today?
I'm in pain.
That's normal. We're giving you medicine to get better. It will just be a few more days.
You'll be fine soon, son.
And you'll see how nice it will be to have you home again.
Excuse me, may I come in?

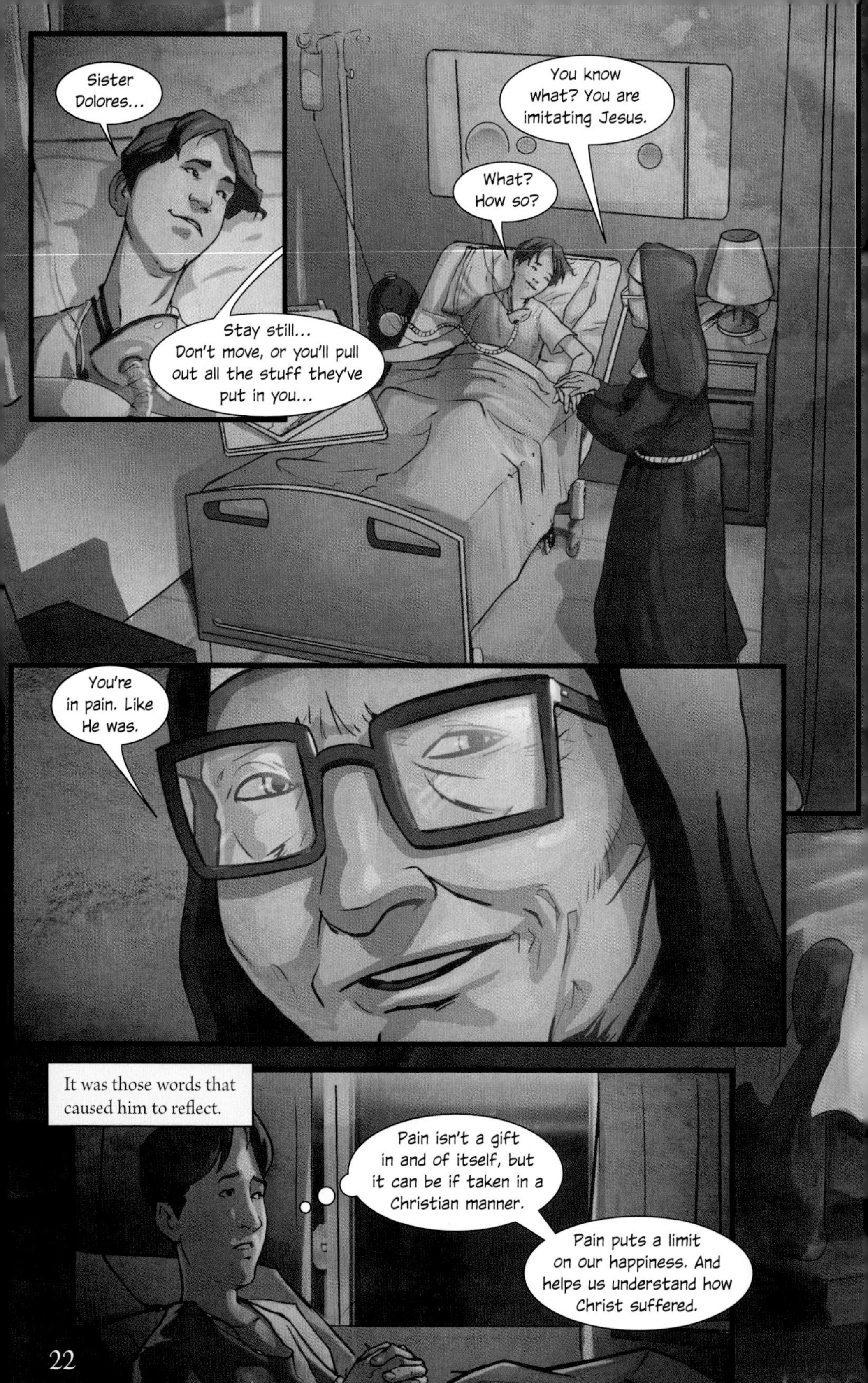

Sister Dolores…
You know what? You are imitating Jesus.
What? How so?
Stay still… Don't move, or you'll pull out all the stuff they've put in you…
You're in pain. Like He was.
It was those words that caused him to reflect.
Pain isn't a gift in and of itself, but it can be if taken in a Christian manner.
Pain puts a limit on our happiness. And helps us understand how Christ suffered.

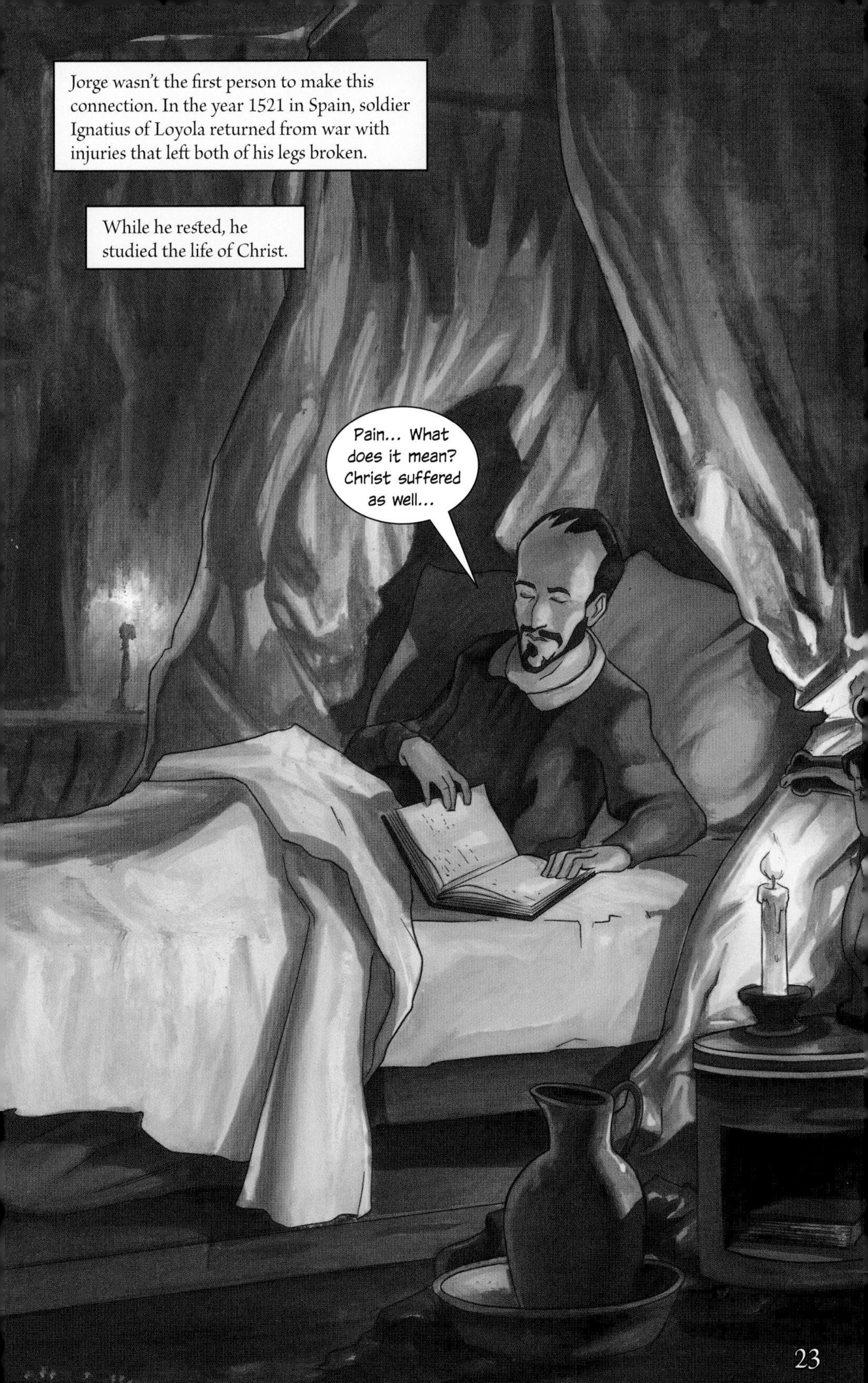
Jorge wasn't the first person to make this connection. In the year 1521 in Spain, soldier Ignatius of Loyola returned from war with injuries that left both of his legs broken.
While he rested, he studied the life of Christ.
Pain... What does it mean? Christ suffered as well...

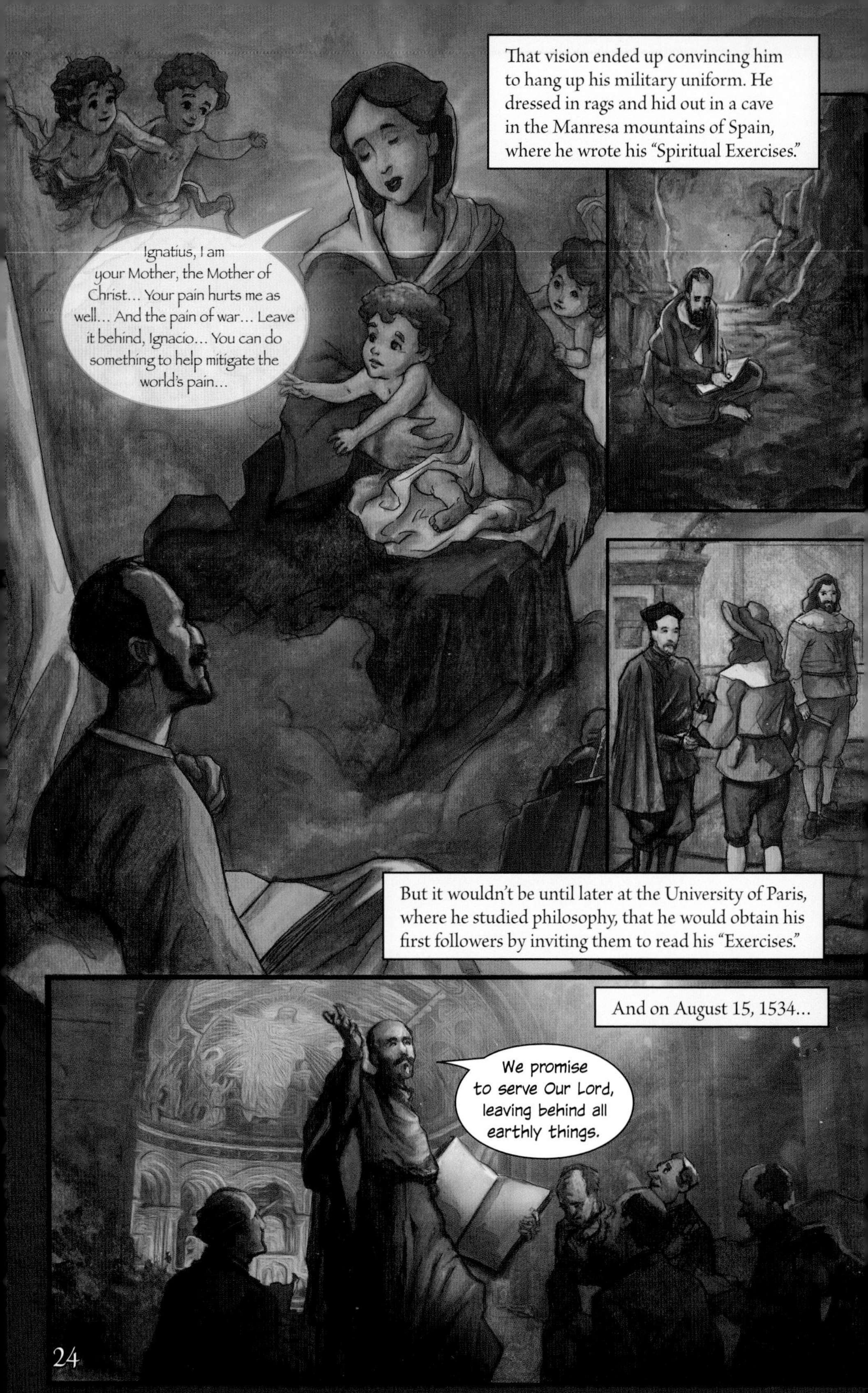
That vision ended up convincing him to hang up his military uniform. He dressed in rags and hid out in a cave in the Manresa mountains of Spain, where he wrote his "Spiritual Exercises."
Ignatius, I am your Mother, the Mother of Christ... Your pain hurts me as well... And the pain of war... Leave it behind, Ignacio... You can do something to help mitigate the world's pain...
But it wouldn't be until later at the University of Paris, where he studied philosophy, that he would obtain his first followers by inviting them to read his "Exercises."
And on August 15, 1534...
We promise to serve Our Lord, leaving behind all earthly things.

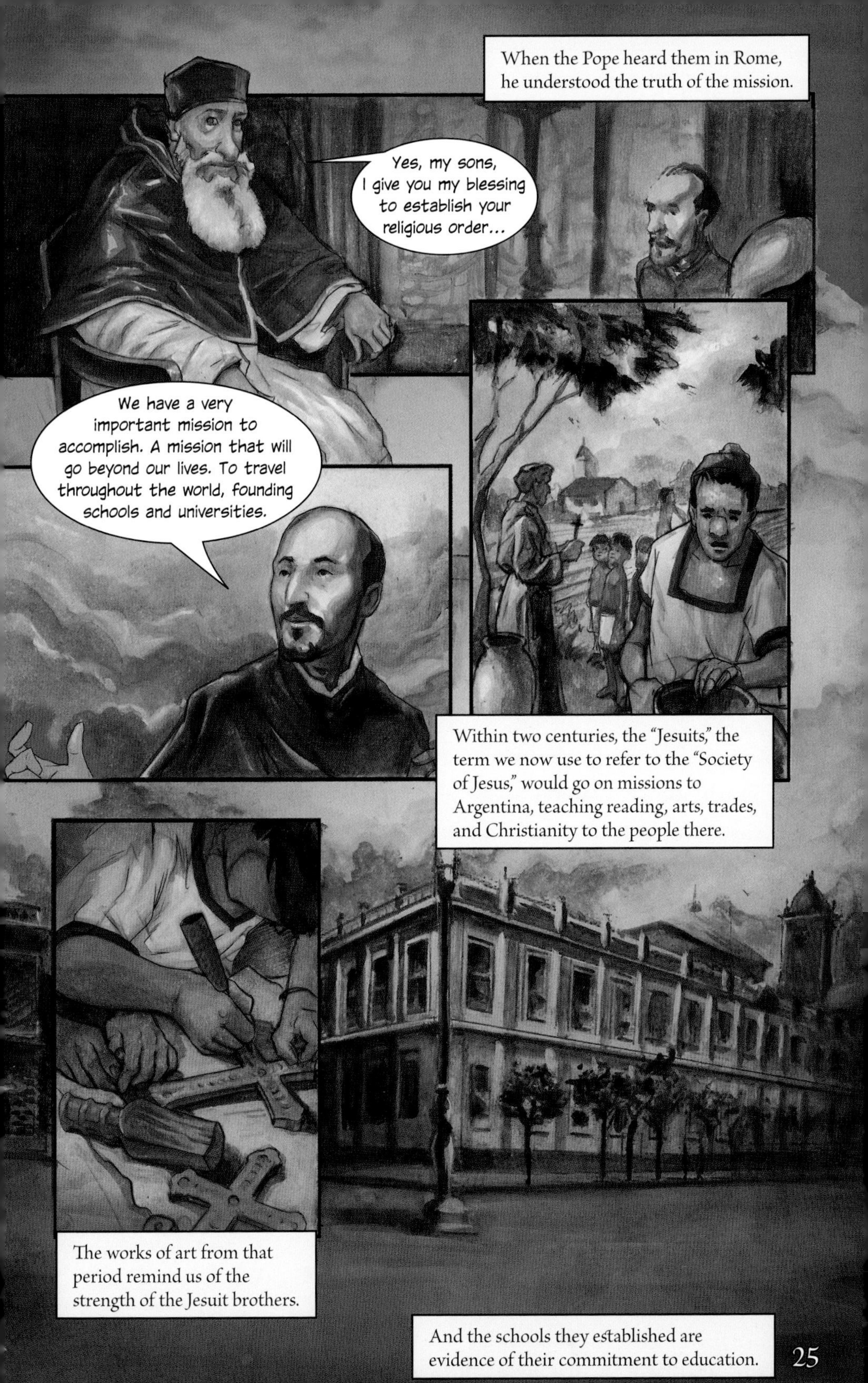
When the Pope heard them in Rome, he understood the truth of the mission.
Yes, my sons, I give you my blessing to establish your religious order...
We have a very important mission to accomplish. A mission that will go beyond our lives. To travel throughout the world, founding schools and universities.
Within two centuries, the "Jesuits," the term we now use to refer to the "Society of Jesus," would go on missions to Argentina, teaching reading, arts, trades, and Christianity to the people there.
The works of art from that period remind us of the strength of the Jesuit brothers.
And the schools they established are evidence of their commitment to education.

CHAPTER 3
THE CALLING

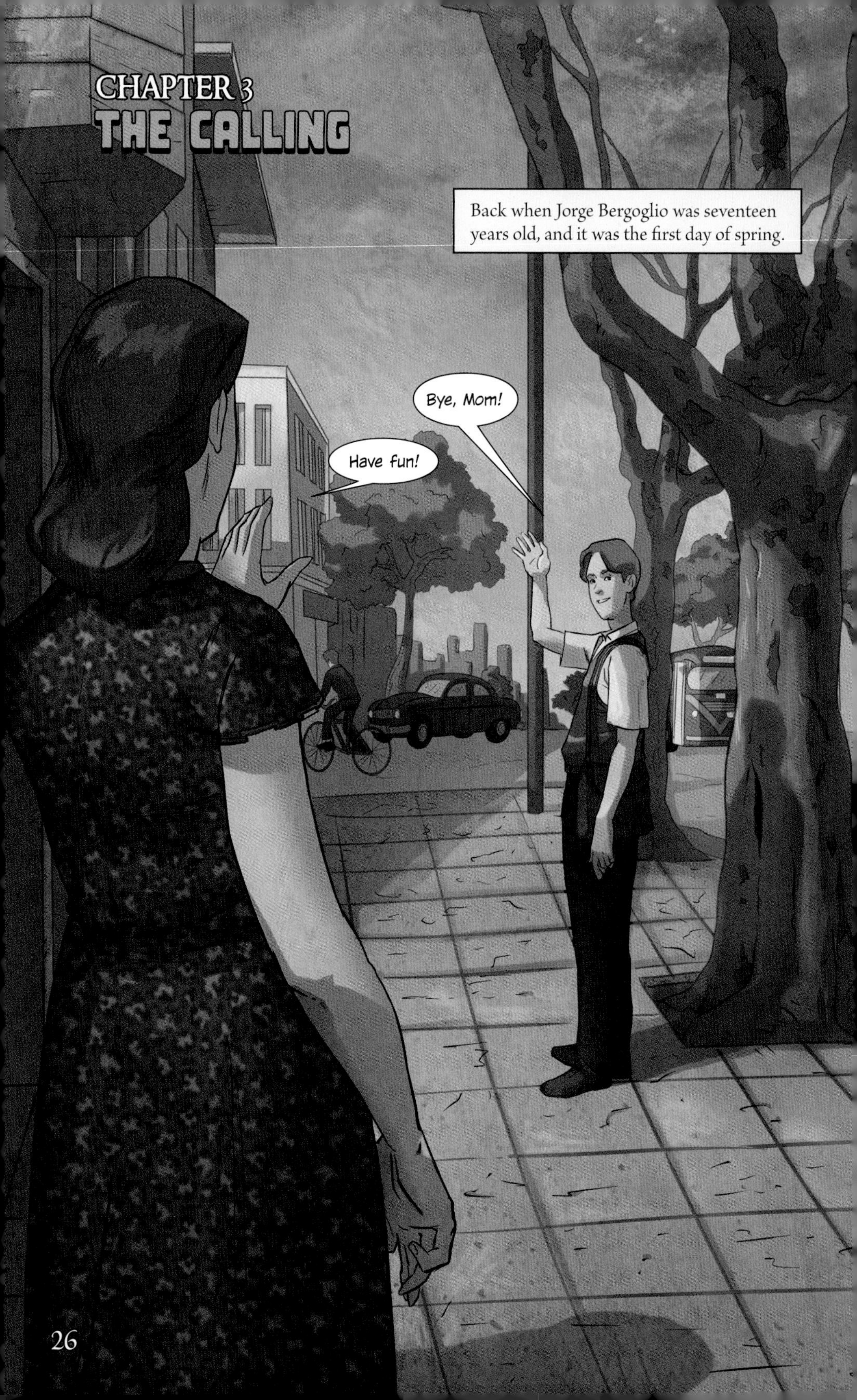
Back when Jorge Bergoglio was seventeen years old, and it was the first day of spring.
Bye, Mom!
Have fun!

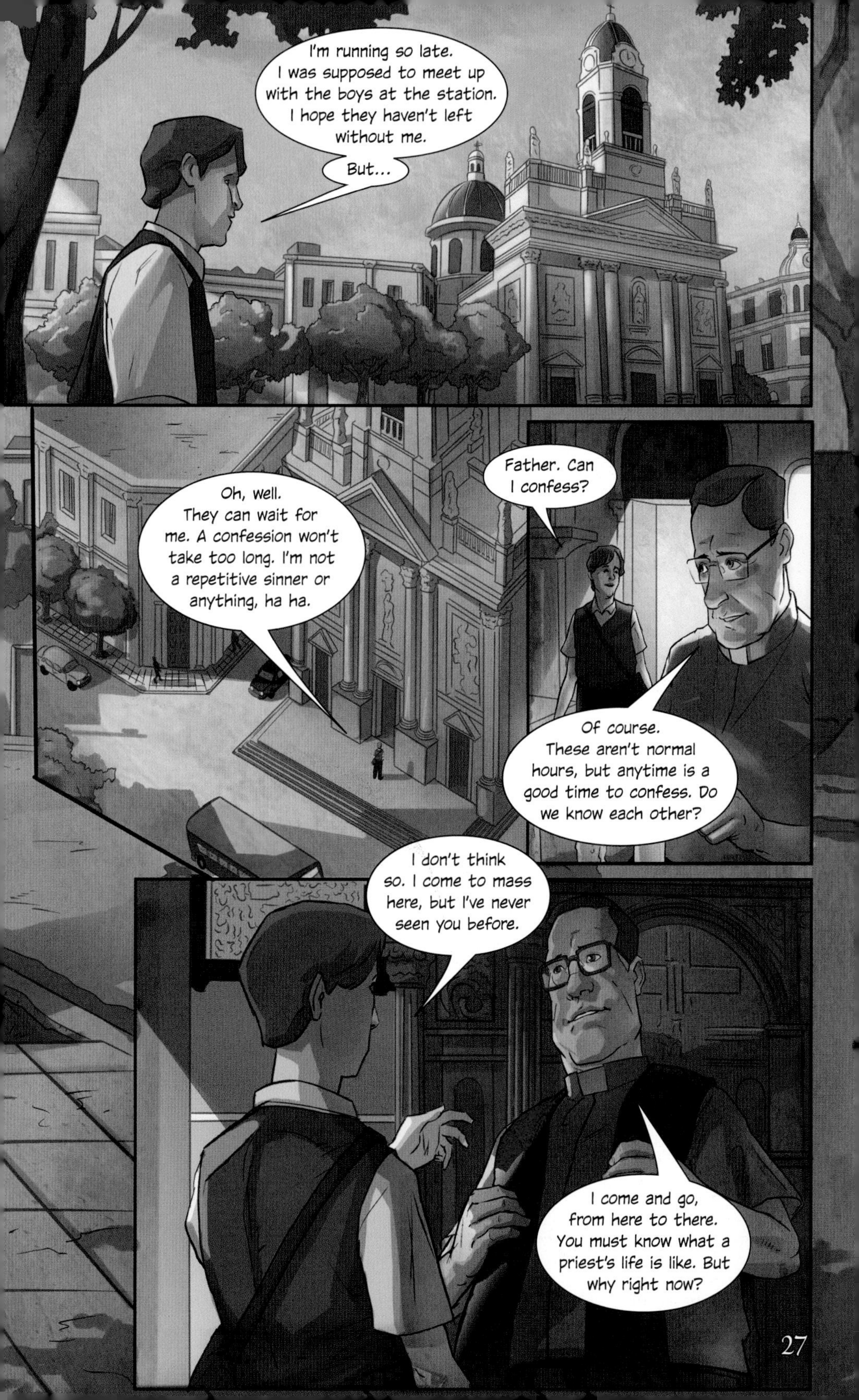

I'm running so late. I was supposed to meet up with the boys at the station. I hope they haven't left without me.
But...
Oh, well. They can wait for me. A confession won't take too long. I'm not a repetitive sinner or anything, ha ha.
Father. Can I confess?
Of course. These aren't normal hours, but anytime is a good time to confess. Do we know each other?
I don't think so. I come to mass here, but I've never seen you before.
I come and go, from here to there. You must know what a priest's life is like. But why right now?

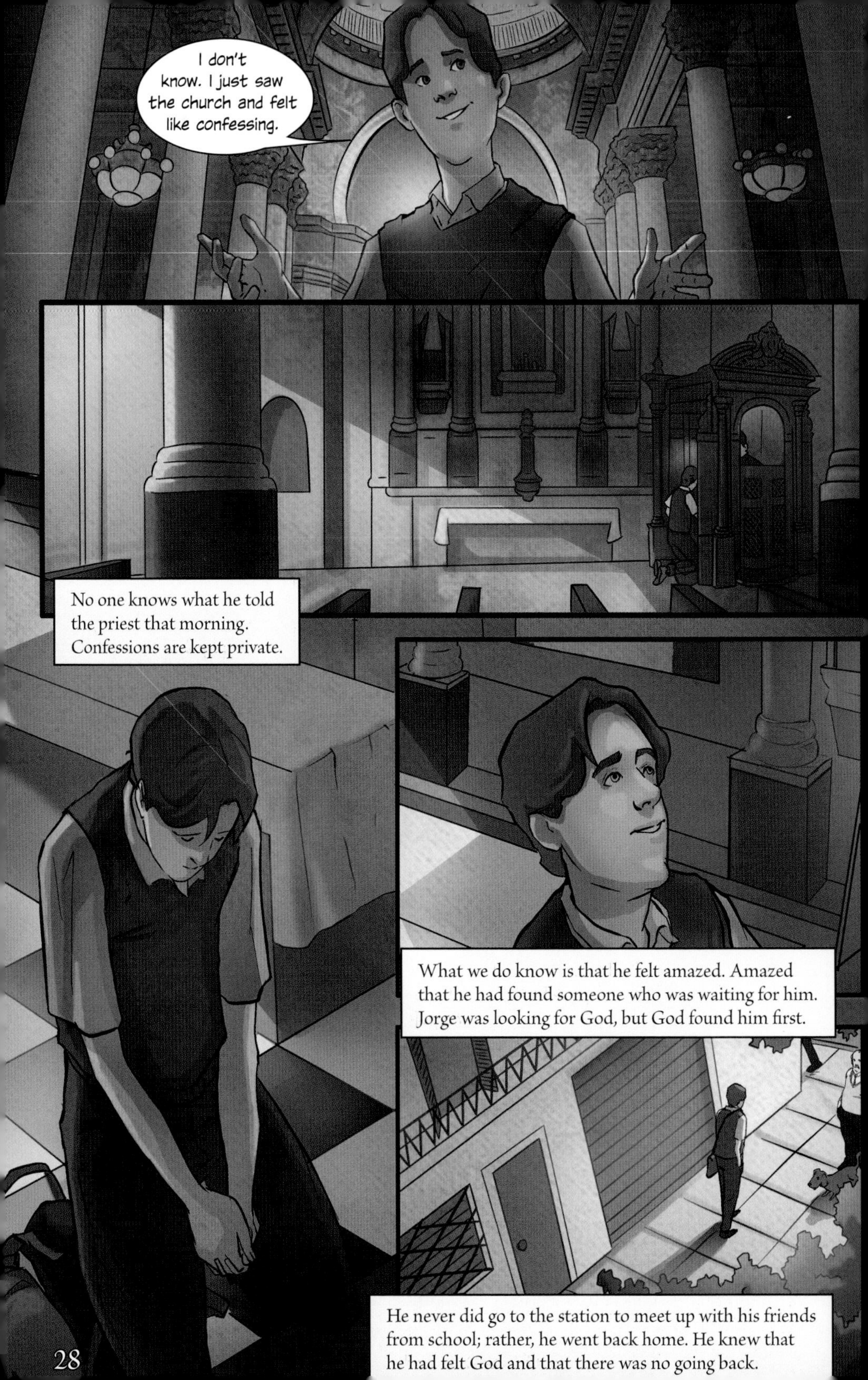

I don't know. I just saw the church and felt like confessing.
No one knows what he told the priest that morning. Confessions are kept private.
What we do know is that he felt amazed. Amazed that he had found someone who was waiting for him. Jorge was looking for God, but God found him first.
He never did go to the station to meet up with his friends from school; rather, he went back home. He knew that he had felt God and that there was no going back.

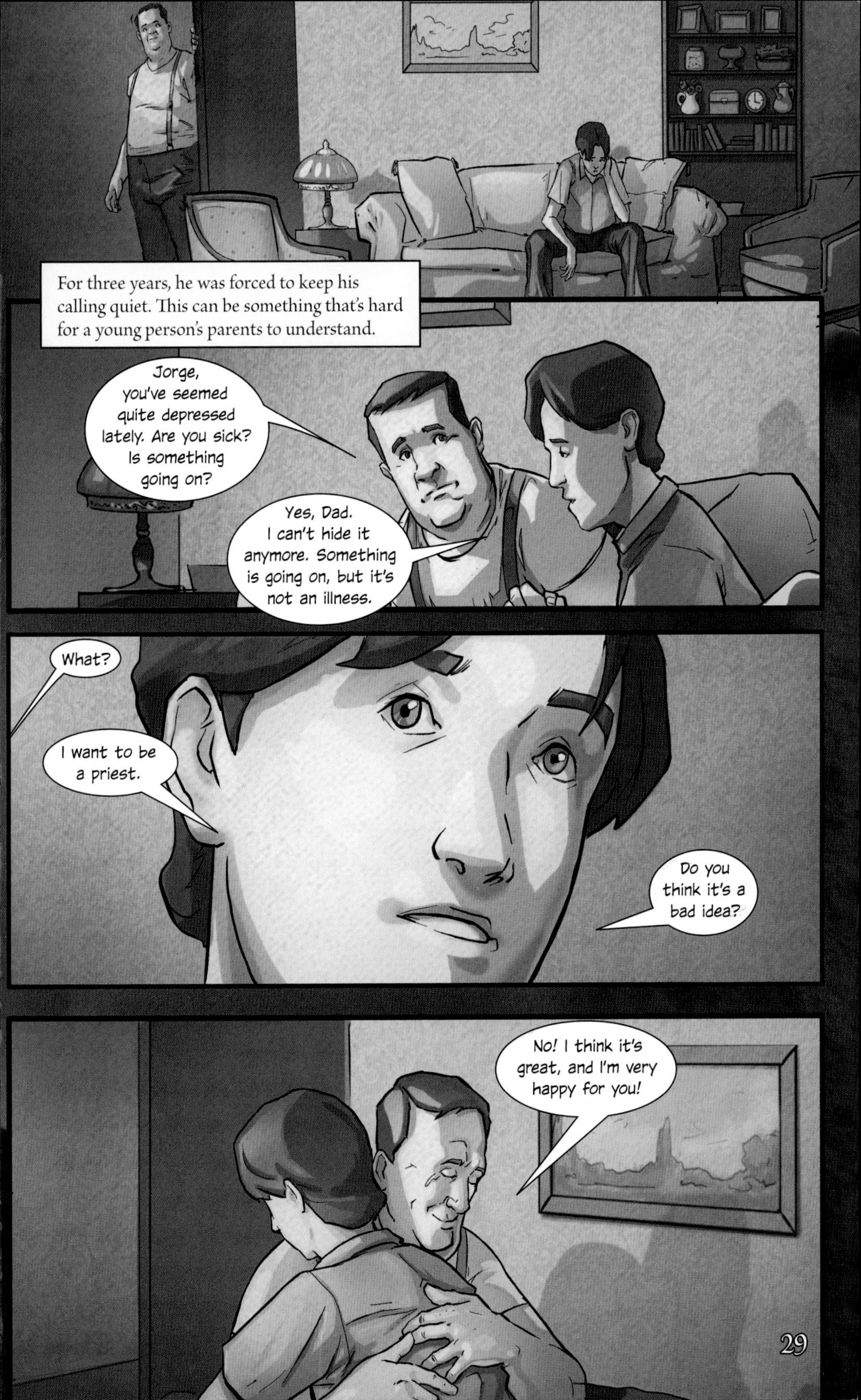
For three years, he was forced to keep his calling quiet. This can be something that's hard for a young person's parents to understand.
Jorge, you've seemed quite depressed lately. Are you sick? Is something going on?
Yes, Dad. I can't hide it anymore. Something is going on, but it's not an illness.
What?
I want to be a priest.
Do you think it's a bad idea?
No! I think it's great, and I'm very happy for you!

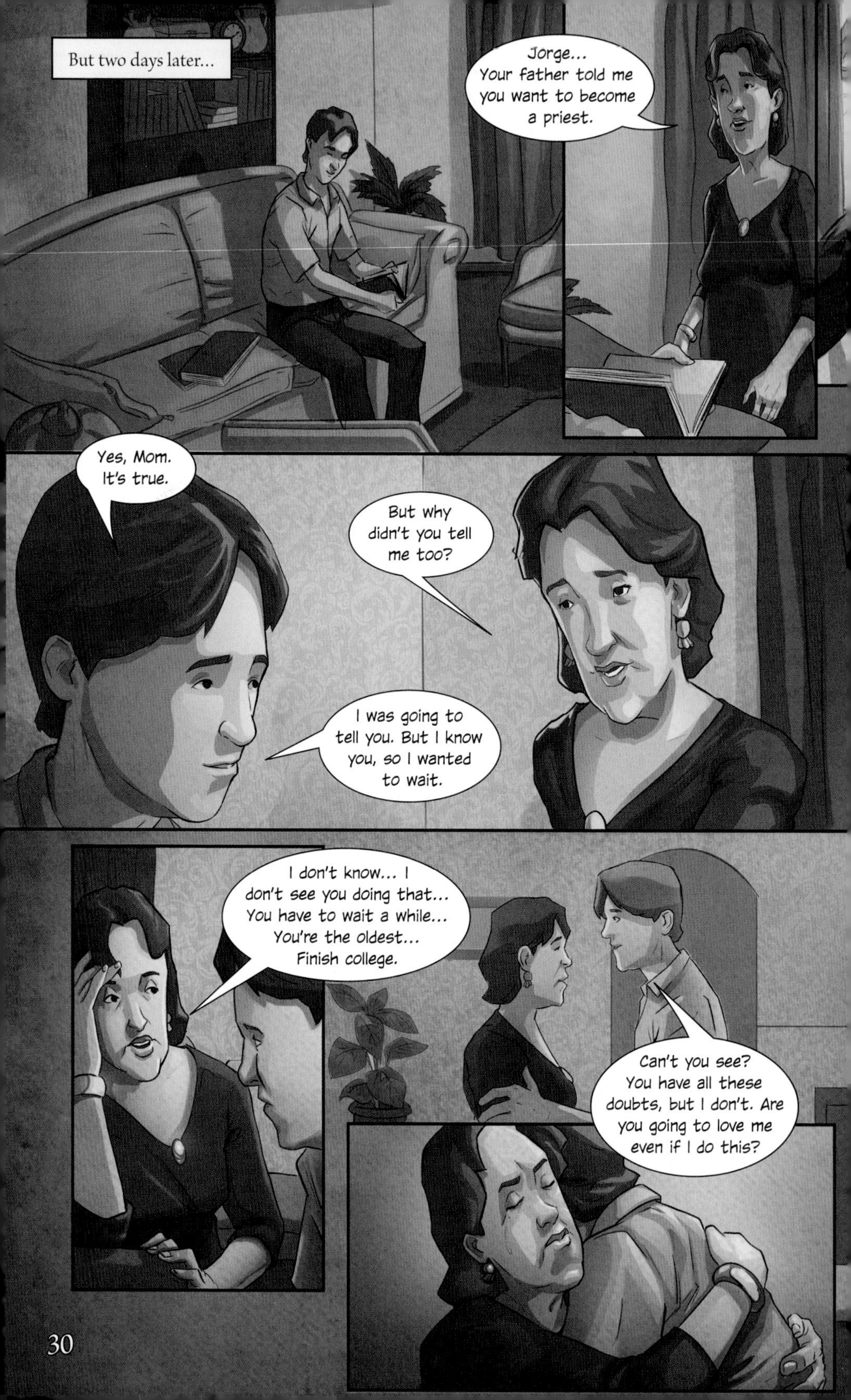
But two days later...
Jorge... Your father told me you want to become a priest.
Yes, Mom. It's true.
But why didn't you tell me too?
I was going to tell you. But I know you, so I wanted to wait.
I don't know... I don't see you doing that... You have to wait a while... You're the oldest... Finish college.
Can't you see? You have all these doubts, but I don't. Are you going to love me even if I do this?

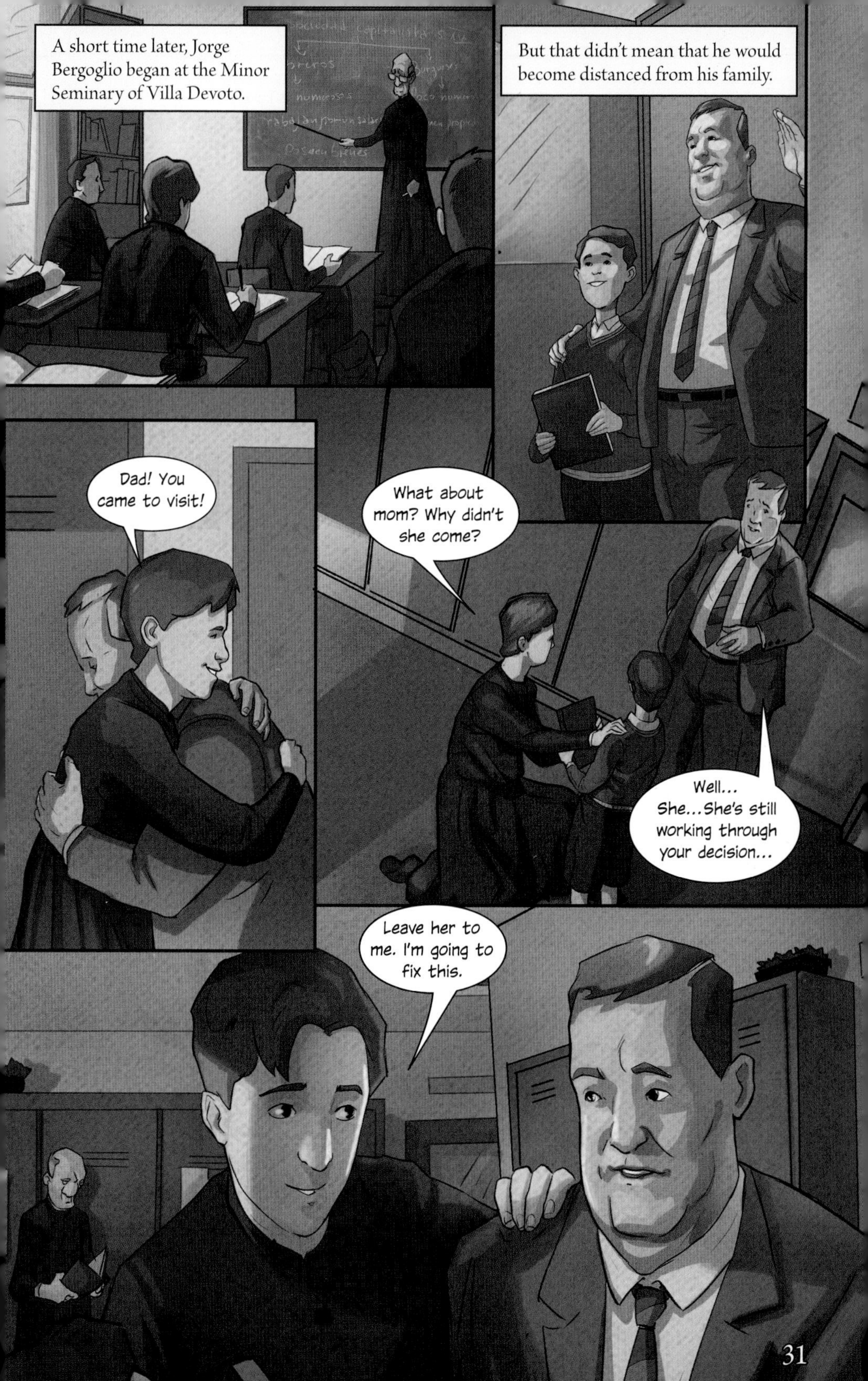
A short time later, Jorge Bergoglio began at the Minor Seminary of Villa Devoto.
But that didn't mean that he would become distanced from his family.
Dad! You came to visit!
What about mom? Why didn't she come?
Well... She...She's still working through your decision...
Leave her to me. I'm going to fix this.

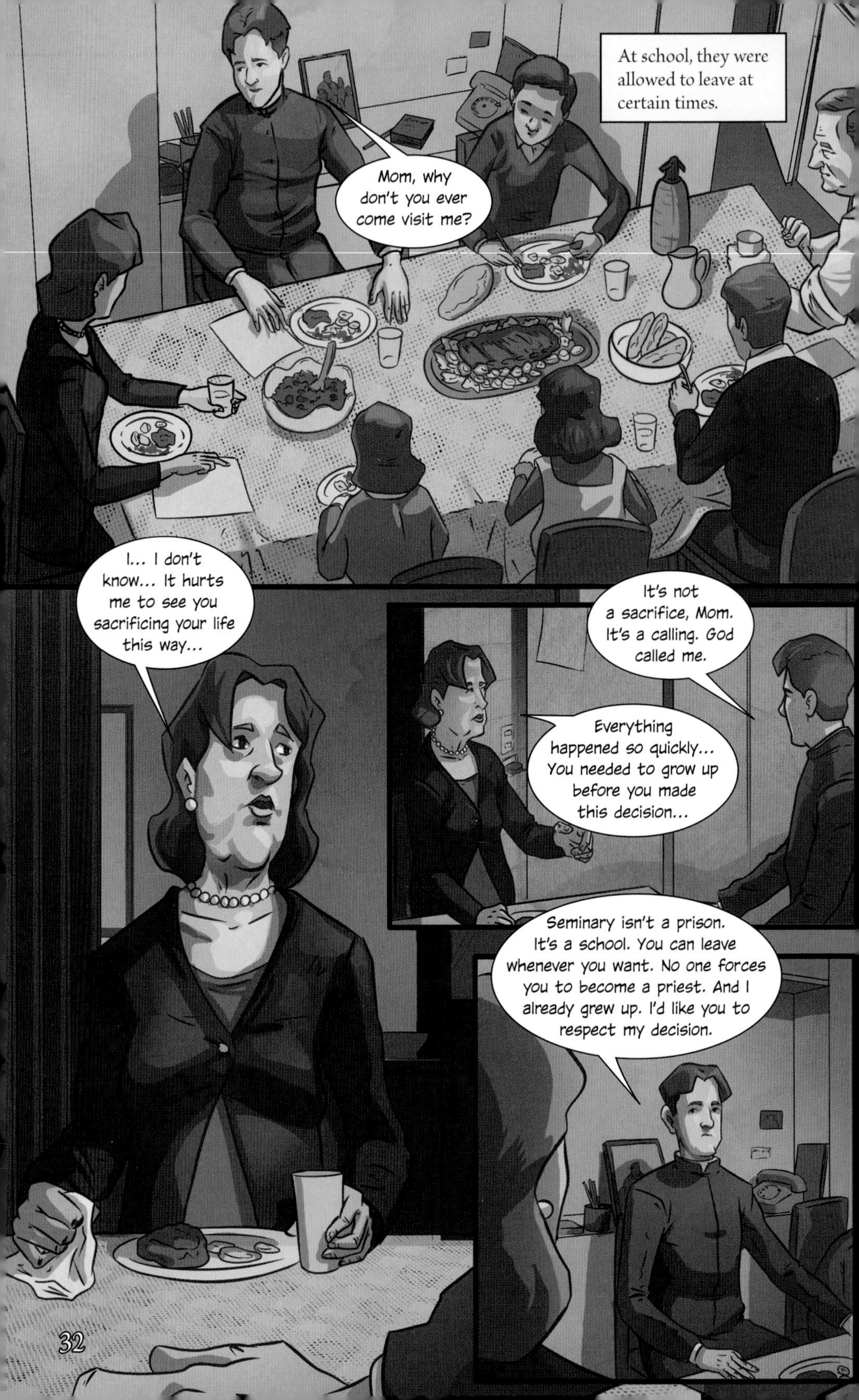
At school, they were allowed to leave at certain times.
Mom, why don't you ever come visit me?
I... I don't know... It hurts me to see you sacrificing your life this way...
It's not a sacrifice, Mom. It's a calling. God called me.
Everything happened so quickly... You needed to grow up before you made this decision...
Seminary isn't a prison. It's a school. You can leave whenever you want. No one forces you to become a priest. And I already grew up. I'd like you to respect my decision.

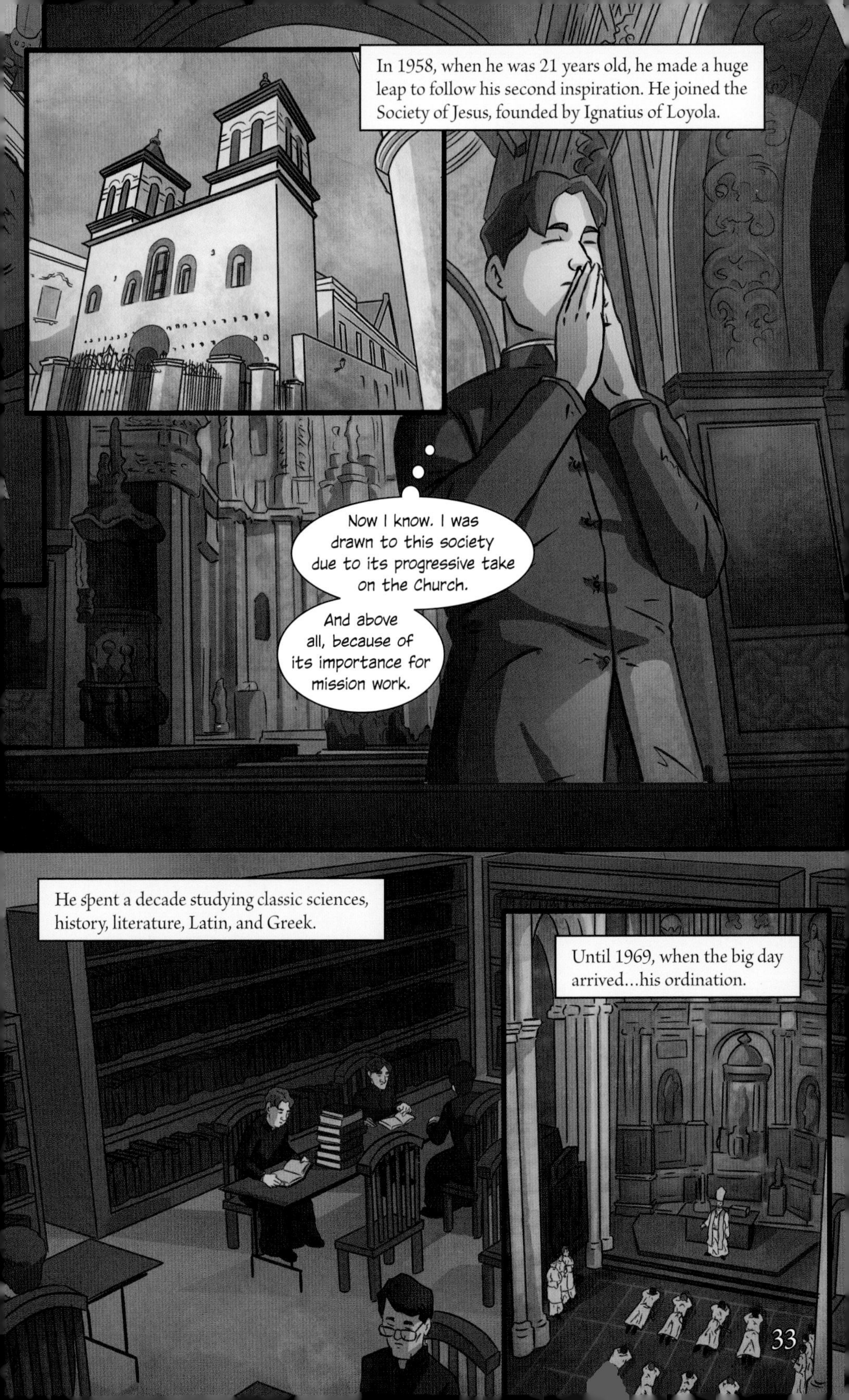
In 1958, when he was 21 years old, he made a huge leap to follow his second inspiration. He joined the Society of Jesus, founded by Ignatius of Loyola.
Now I know. I was drawn to this society due to its progressive take on the Church.
And above all, because of its importance for mission work.
He spent a decade studying classic sciences, history, literature, Latin, and Greek.
Until 1969, when the big day arrived...his ordination.

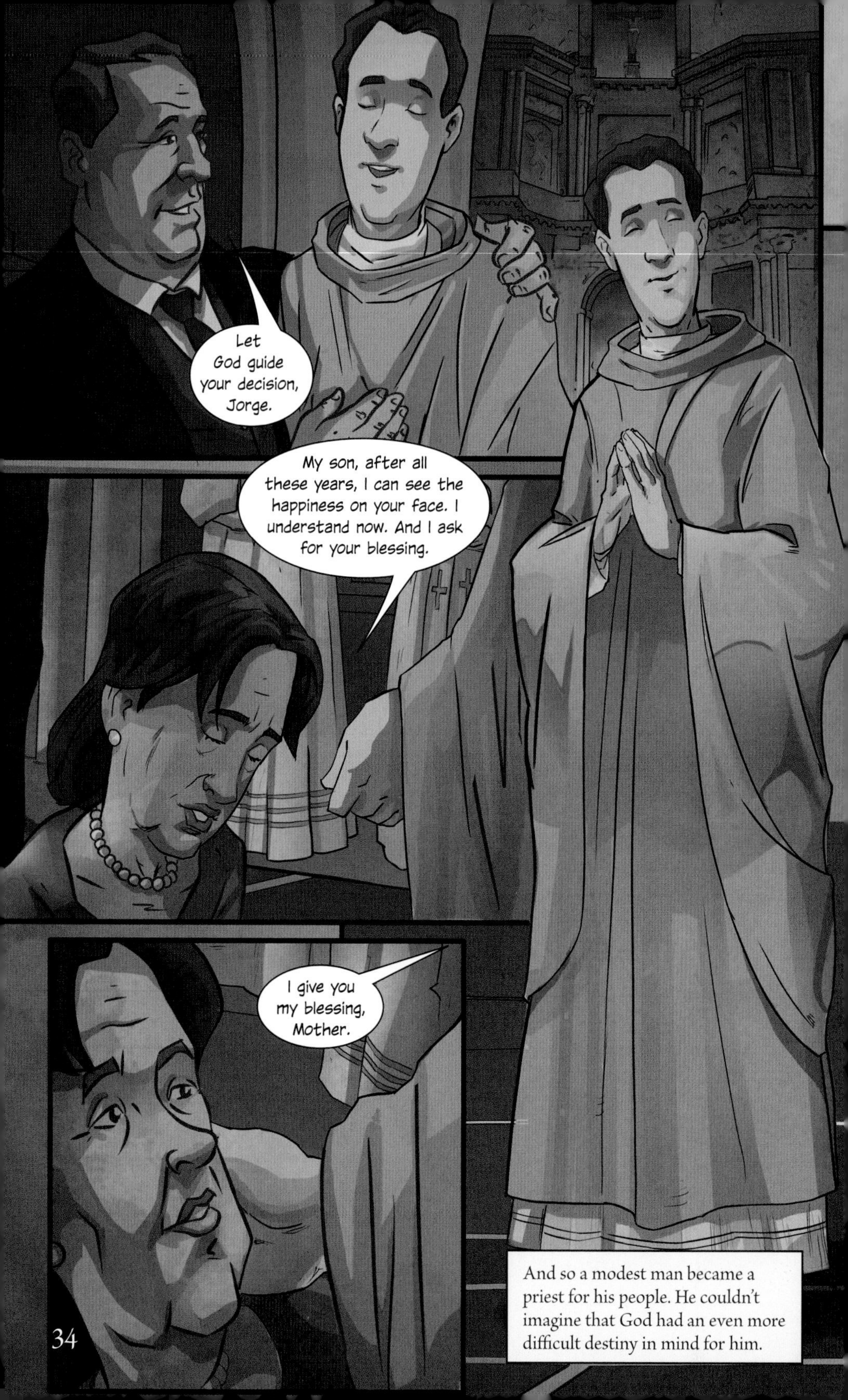
Let God guide your decision, Jorge.
My son, after all these years, I can see the happiness on your face. I understand now. And I ask for your blessing.
I give you my blessing, Mother.
And so a modest man became a priest for his people. He couldn't imagine that God had an even more difficult destiny in mind for him.

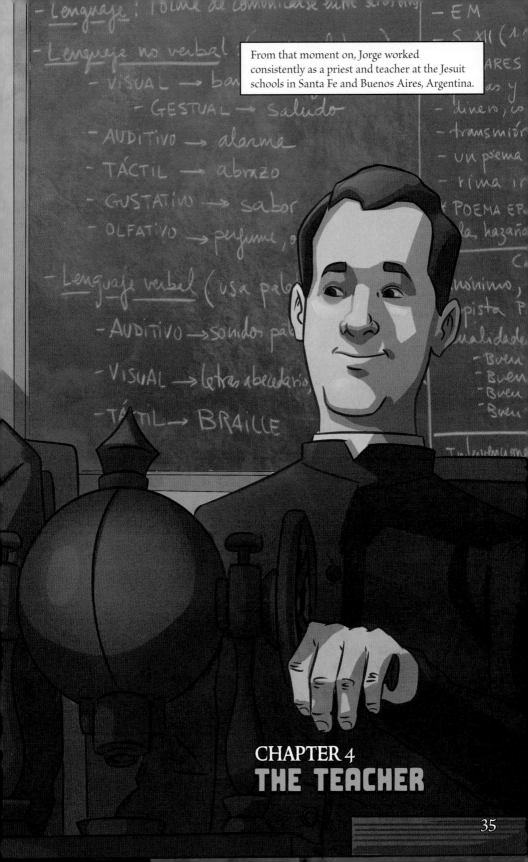

From that moment on, Jorge worked consistently as a priest and teacher at the Jesuit schools in Santa Fe and Buenos Aires, Argentina.

CHAPTER 4
THE TEACHER

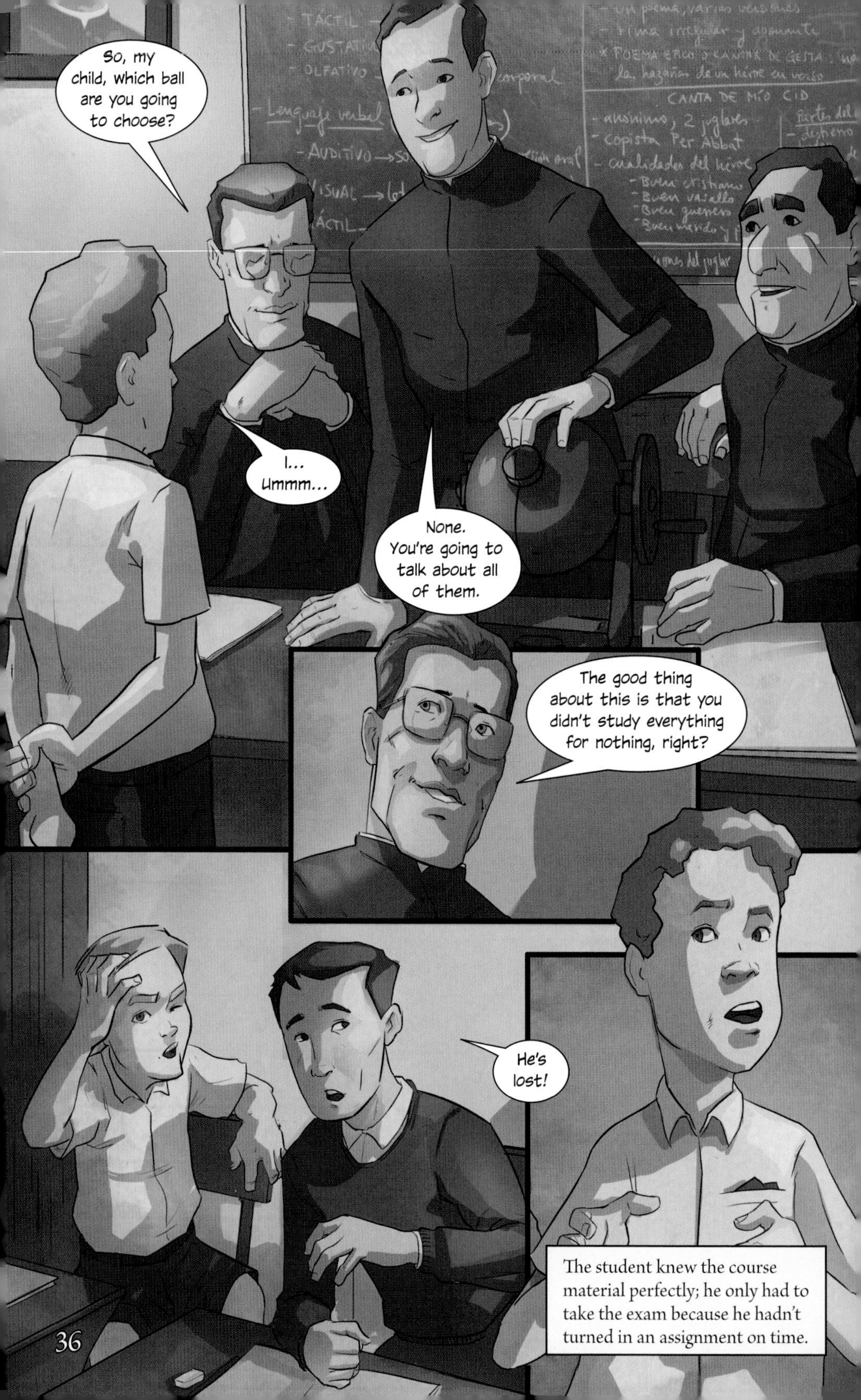
So, my child, which ball are you going to choose?
I... Ummm...
None. You're going to talk about all of them.
The good thing about this is that you didn't study everything for nothing, right?
He's lost!
The student knew the course material perfectly; he only had to take the exam because he hadn't turned in an assignment on time.
CANTA DE MÍO CID
- copista Per Abbat
- Buen cristiano
- Buen vasallo
- Buen guerrero

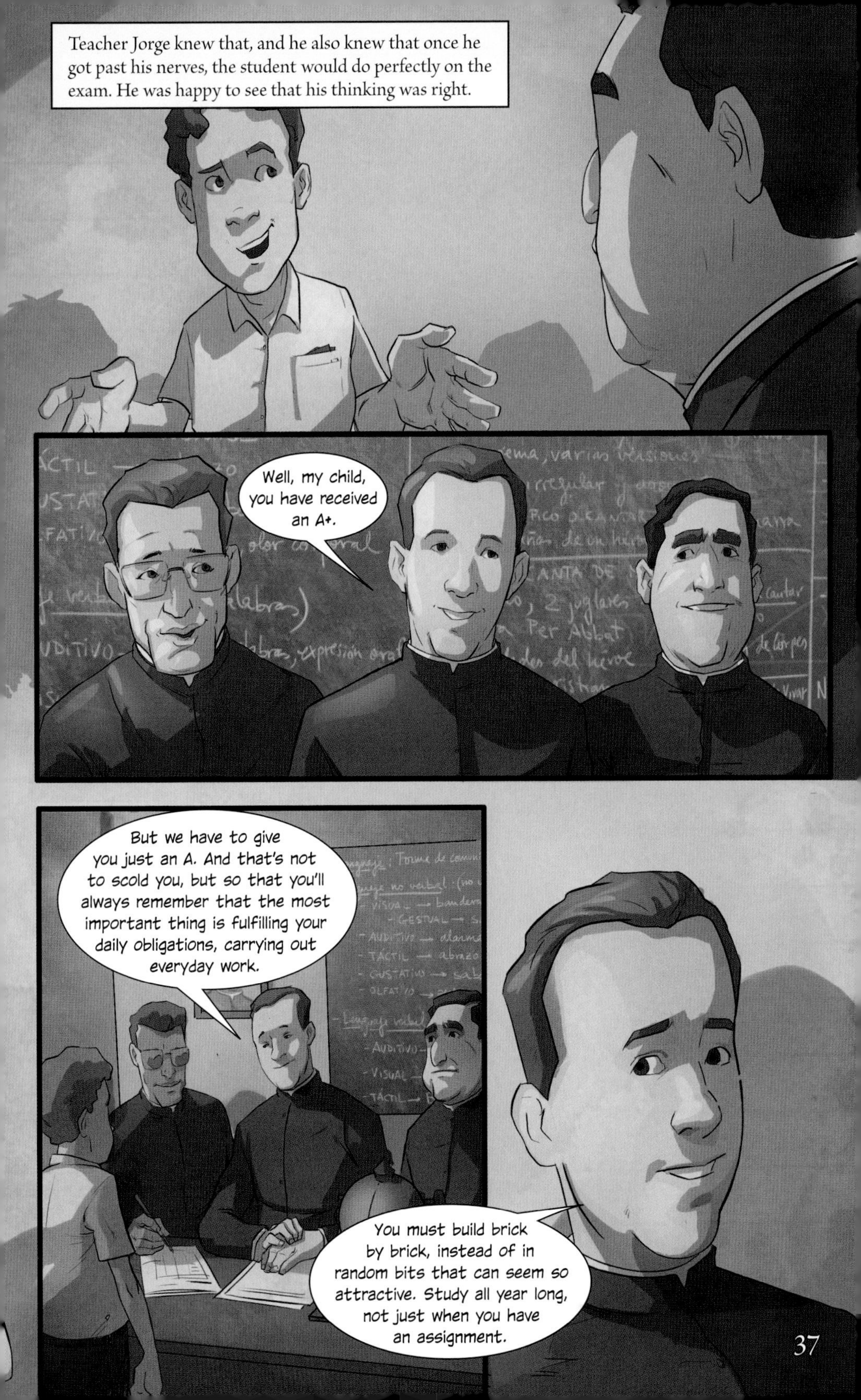
Teacher Jorge knew that, and he also knew that once he got past his nerves, the student would do perfectly on the exam. He was happy to see that his thinking was right.
Well, my child, you have received an A+.
But we have to give you just an A. And that's not to scold you, but so that you'll always remember that the most important thing is fulfilling your daily obligations, carrying out everyday work.
You must build brick by brick, instead of in random bits that can seem so attractive. Study all year long, not just when you have an assignment.

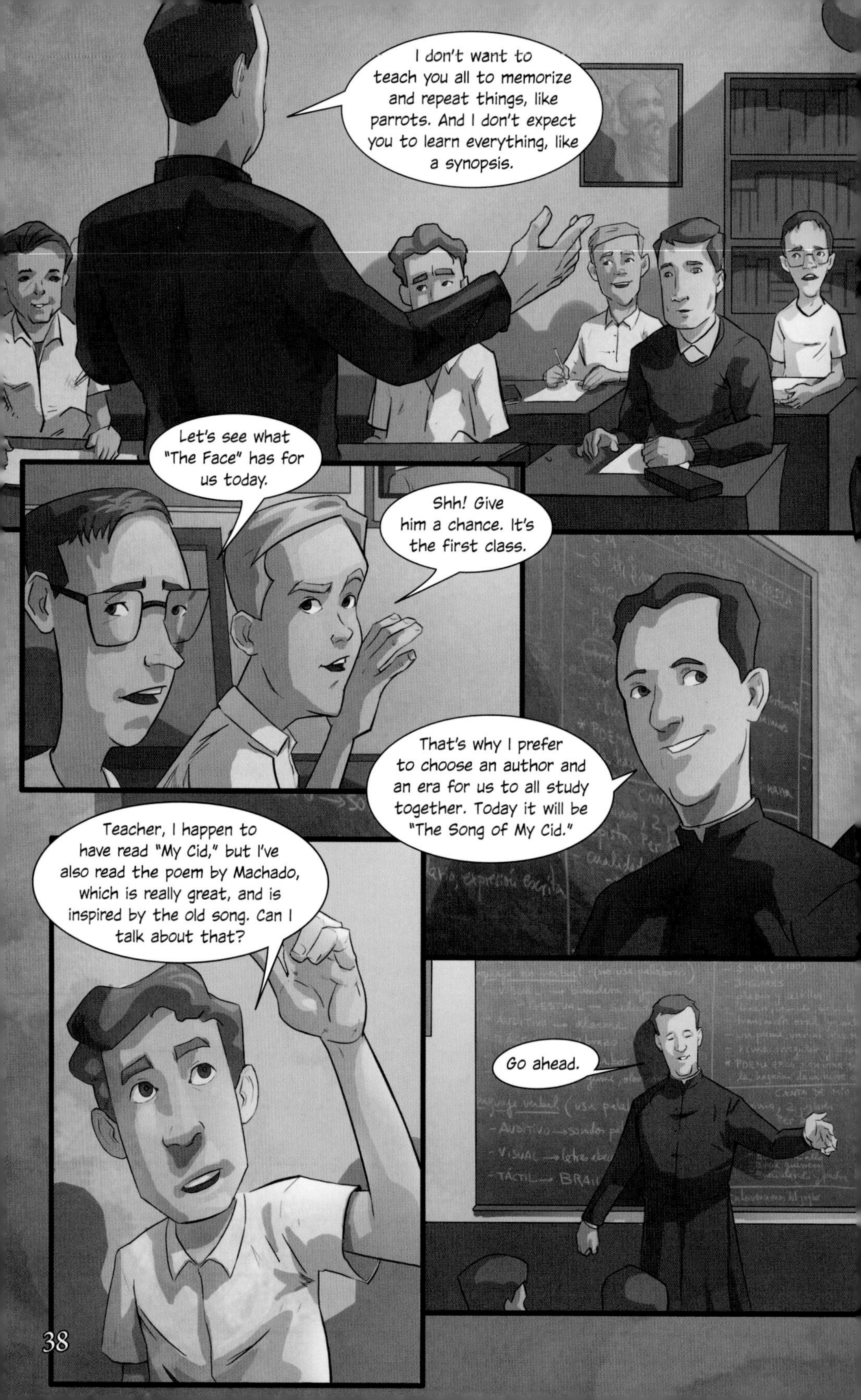
I don't want to teach you all to memorize and repeat things, like parrots. And I don't expect you to learn everything, like a synopsis.
Let's see what "The Face" has for us today.
Shh! Give him a chance. It's the first class.
That's why I prefer to choose an author and an era for us to all study together. Today it will be "The Song of My Cid."
Teacher, I happen to have read "My Cid," but I've also read the poem by Machado, which is really great, and is inspired by the old song. Can I talk about that?
Go ahead.

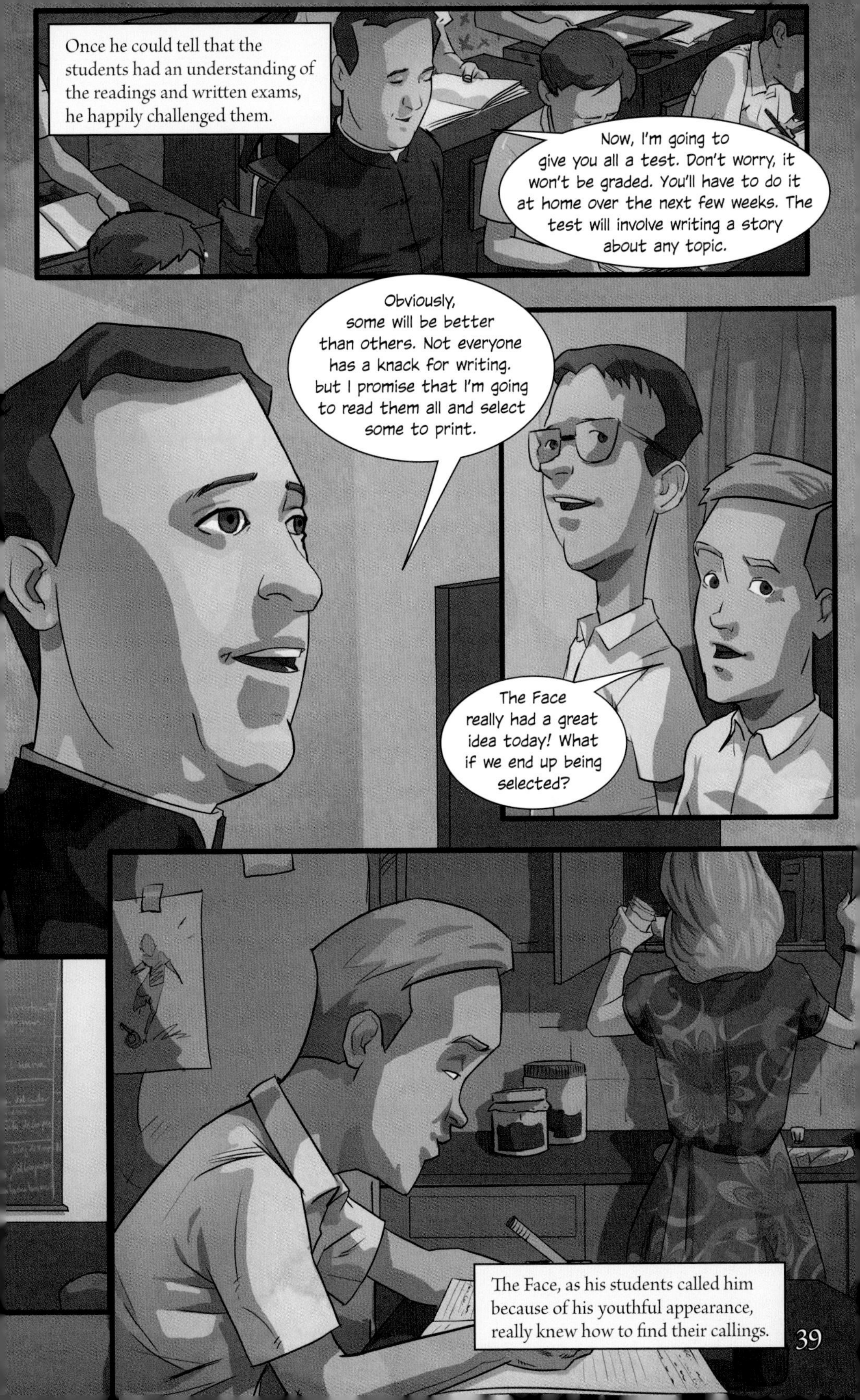
Once he could tell that the students had an understanding of the readings and written exams, he happily challenged them.
Now, I'm going to give you all a test. Don't worry, it won't be graded. You'll have to do it at home over the next few weeks. The test will involve writing a story about any topic.
Obviously, some will be better than others. Not everyone has a knack for writing. but I promise that I'm going to read them all and select some to print.
The Face really had a great idea today! What if we end up being selected?
The Face, as his students called him because of his youthful appearance, really knew how to find their callings.

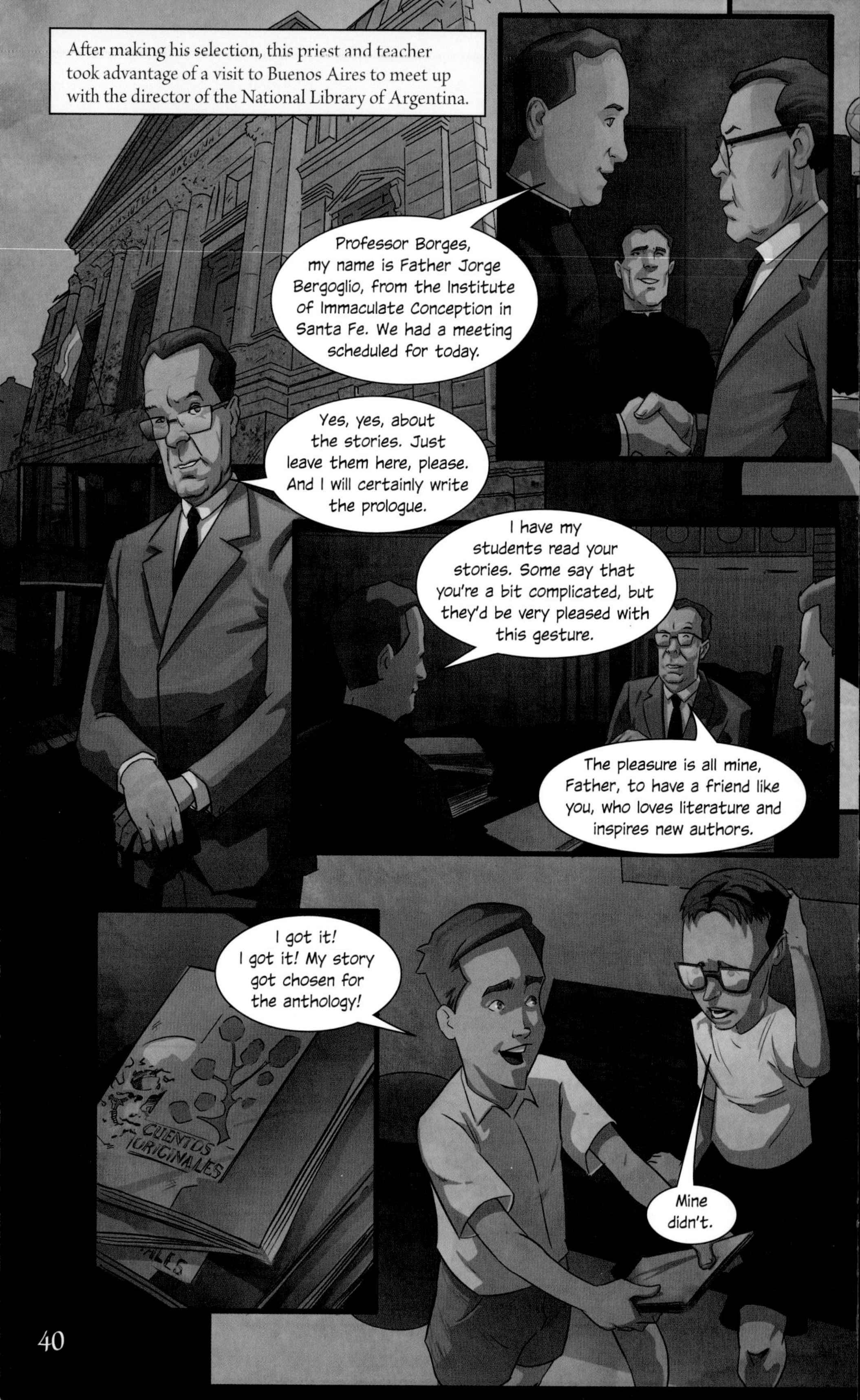
After making his selection, this priest and teacher took advantage of a visit to Buenos Aires to meet up with the director of the National Library of Argentina.
Professor Borges, my name is Father Jorge Bergoglio, from the Institute of Immaculate Conception in Santa Fe. We had a meeting scheduled for today.
Yes, yes, about the stories. Just leave them here, please. And I will certainly write the prologue.
I have my students read your stories. Some say that you're a bit complicated, but they'd be very pleased with this gesture.
The pleasure is all mine, Father, to have a friend like you, who loves literature and inspires new authors.
I got it! I got it! My story got chosen for the anthology!
CUENTOS ORIGINALES
Mine didn't.

Jorge's teaching never faltered.
Very good, Candioti. You have answered all of the questions correctly.
That's not from studying, but because I have a vast range of knowledge about this subject.
Very good. You got an A on the exam, but since you didn't study, I'm giving you an F for the idea.
What?
Between an A and an F, your average is a C. That's your final grade.
Teaching doesn't only involve building knowledge, but values too.

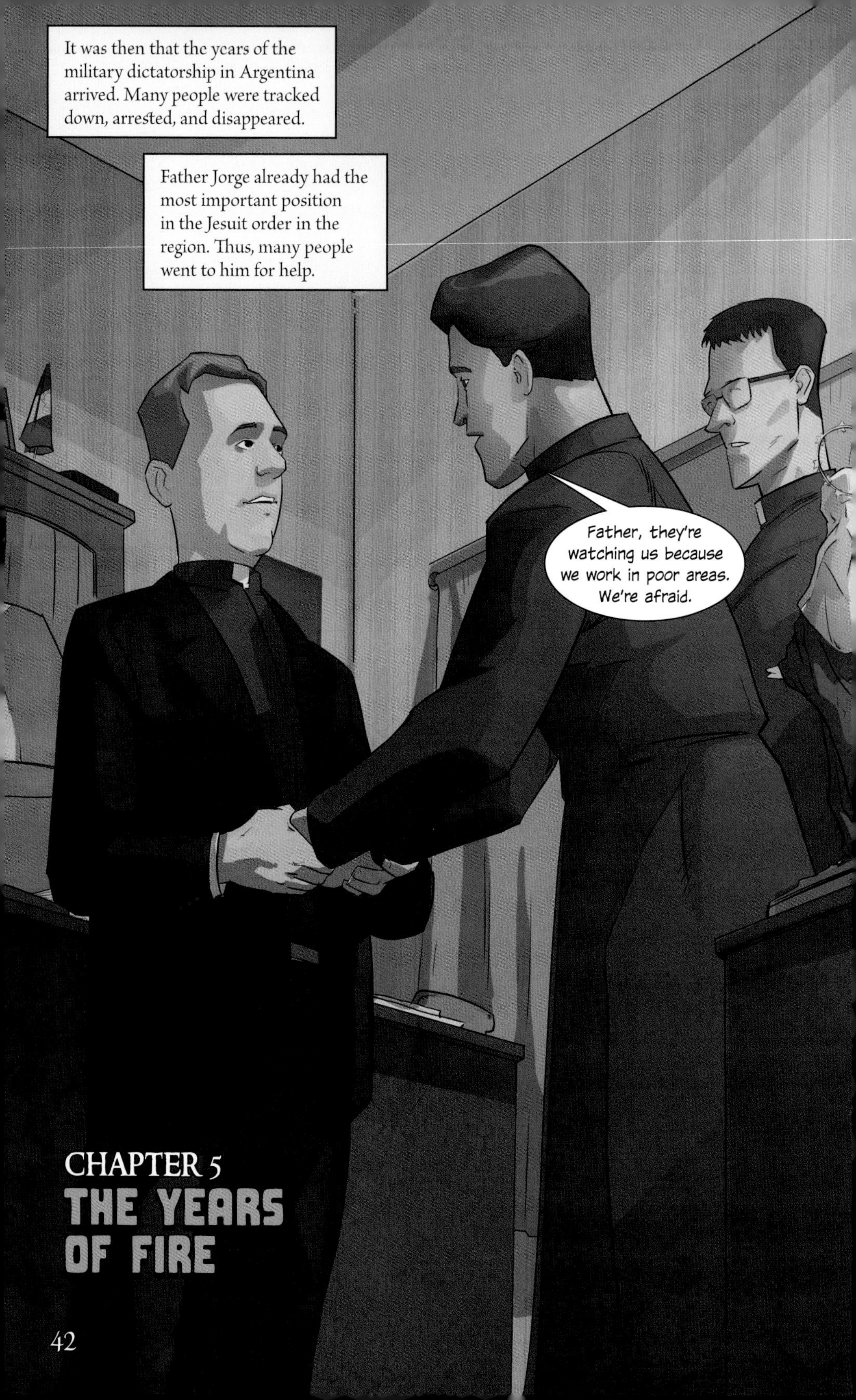
It was then that the years of the military dictatorship in Argentina arrived. Many people were tracked down, arrested, and disappeared.
Father Jorge already had the most important position in the Jesuit order in the region. Thus, many people went to him for help.
Father, they're watching us because we work in poor areas. We're afraid.
CHAPTER 5
THE YEARS OF FIRE

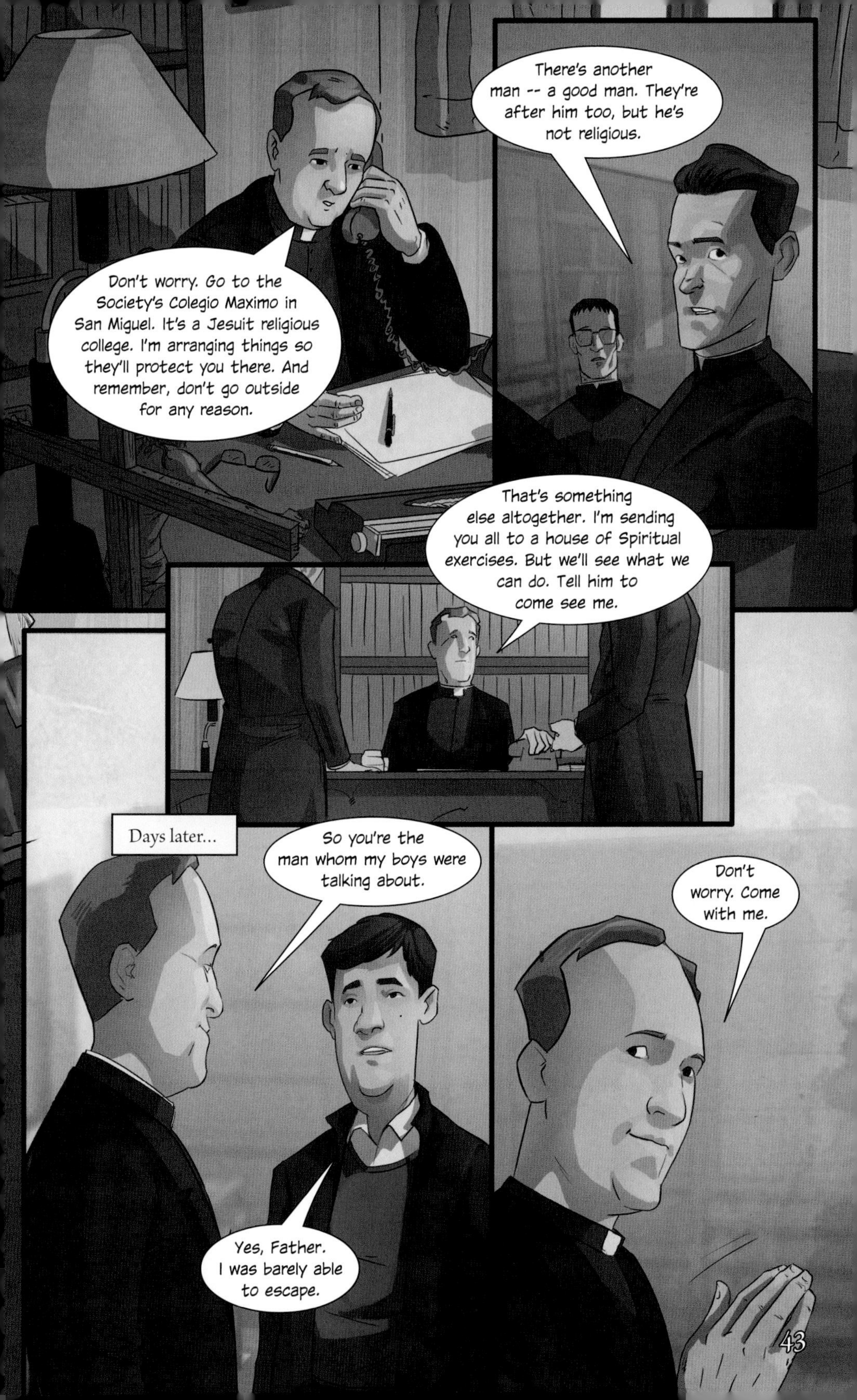

Don't worry. Go to the Society's Colegio Maximo in San Miguel. It's a Jesuit religious college. I'm arranging things so they'll protect you there. And remember, don't go outside for any reason.
There's another man -- a good man. They're after him too, but he's not religious.
That's something else altogether. I'm sending you all to a house of Spiritual exercises. But we'll see what we can do. Tell him to come see me.
Days later...
So you're the man whom my boys were talking about.
Yes, Father. I was barely able to escape.
Don't worry. Come with me.

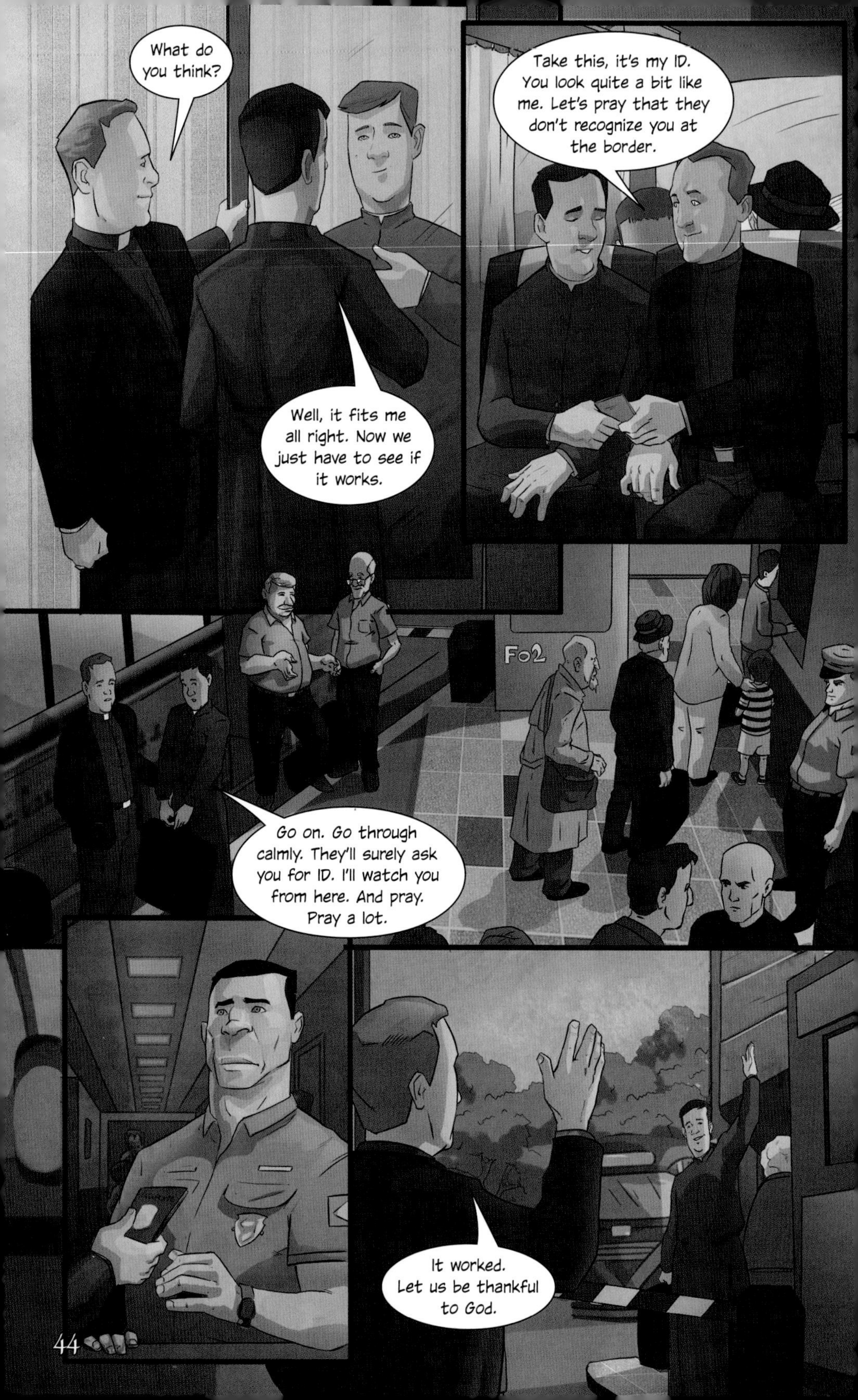
What do you think?
Well, it fits me all right. Now we just have to see if it works.
Take this, it's my ID. You look quite a bit like me. Let's pray that they don't recognize you at the border.
Fo2
Go on. Go through calmly. They'll surely ask you for ID. I'll watch you from here. And pray. Pray a lot.
It worked. Let us be thankful to God.

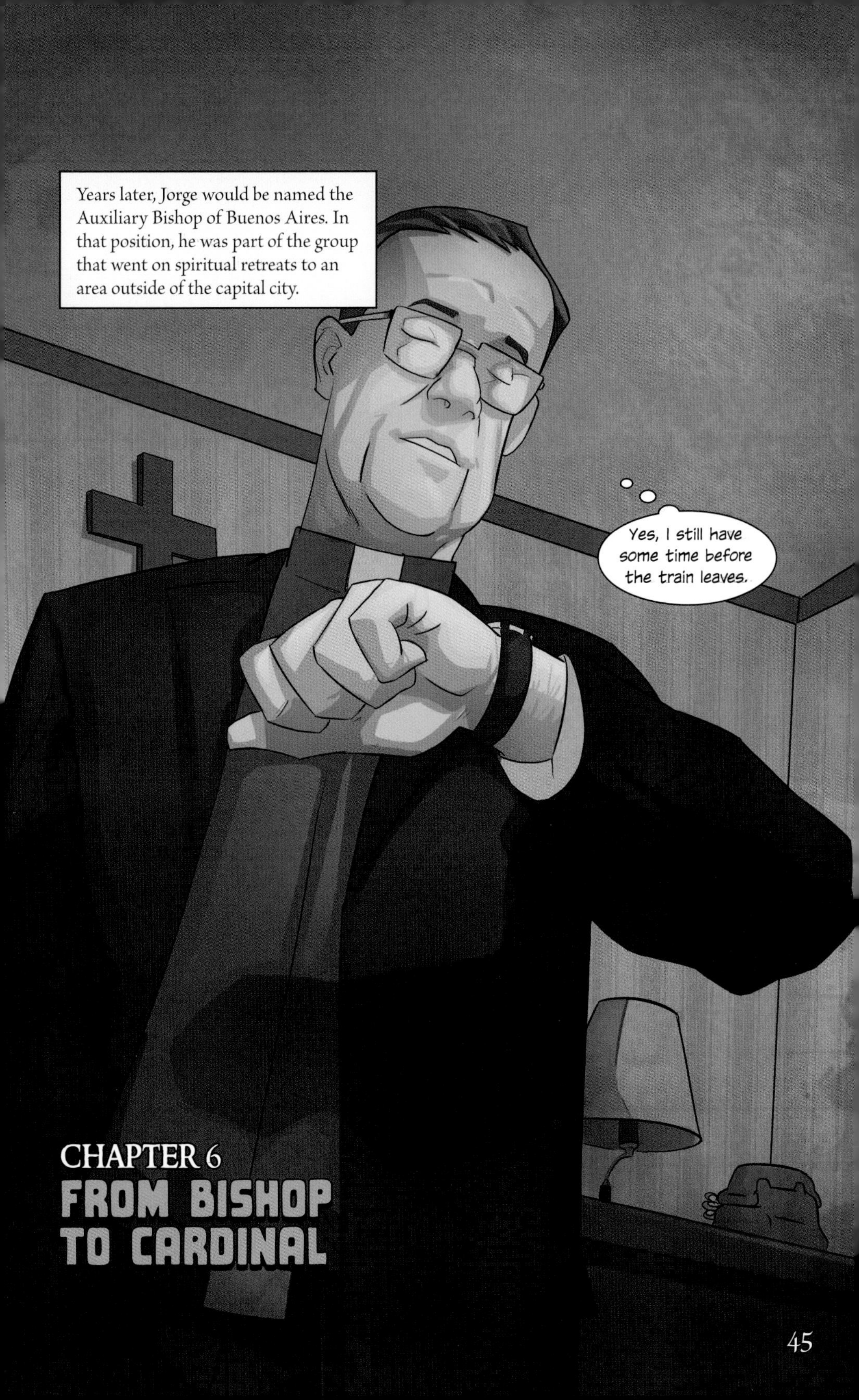
Years later, Jorge would be named the Auxiliary Bishop of Buenos Aires. In that position, he was part of the group that went on spiritual retreats to an area outside of the capital city.
Yes, I still have some time before the train leaves.

CHAPTER 6
FROM BISHOP TO CARDINAL

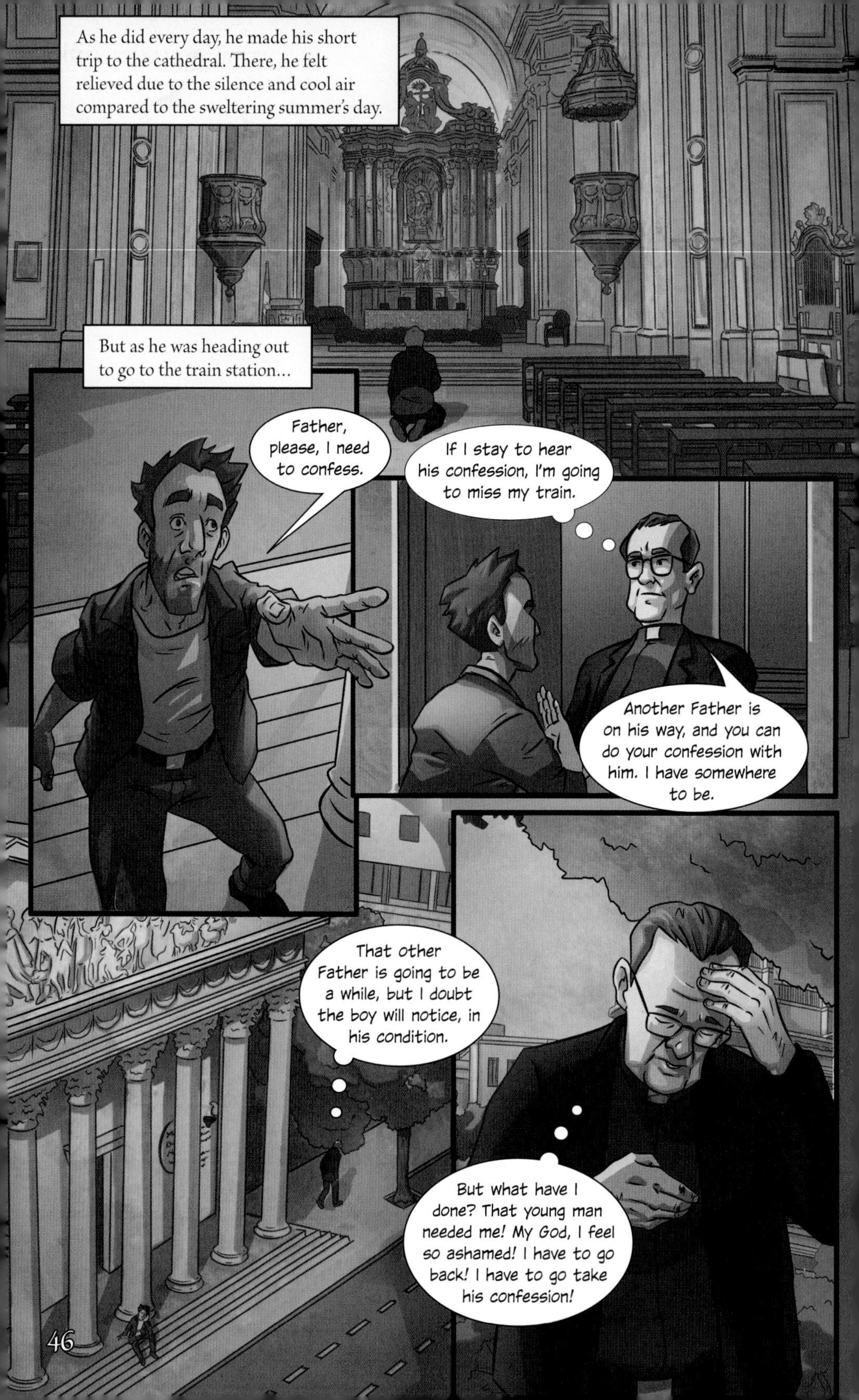
As he did every day, he made his short trip to the cathedral. There, he felt relieved due to the silence and cool air compared to the sweltering summer's day.
But as he was heading out to go to the train station...
Father, please, I need to confess.
If I stay to hear his confession, I'm going to miss my train.
Another Father is on his way, and you can do your confession with him. I have somewhere to be.
That other Father is going to be a while, but I doubt the boy will notice, in his condition.
But what have I done? That young man needed me! My God, I feel so ashamed! I have to go back! I have to go take his confession!

And so he did.

Then, he took him in front of the Virgin Mary.

Blessed Mother of God, take care of this young man.

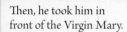
And when he arrived at the station...

Yes, I'm several minutes late. The train is already gone.

Passengers: the 3:30 p.m. train has been delayed. Your new scheduled departure time is 4:00 p.m. Thank you.

And when he returned from the spiritual retreat, before going home...

Father, I needed to confess this. I've realized that god's power has no limits.

47

In 1998, after the death of Father Quarracino, Jorge was named Archbishop of Buenos Aires. But it isn't until he turns 65 years old that he received some very special news.
What do you mean? That can't be true!
Yes, Father. Pope John Paul II is going to name you a Cardinal. I'm going to start preparing the arrangements right now.
Hold on a second. What arrangements are you talking about?
You need new robes.
Forget about that. I'm not being named cardinal just so I can go waste money. I'll wear my old Father robes.
Did you hear, Father? Hundreds of worshippers are going to travel to Rome to be at your ceremony.
What?
Issue this statement: "Bishop Bergoglio thanks you for wanting to be present at the ceremony, but he suggests that you donate that money to help the needy."

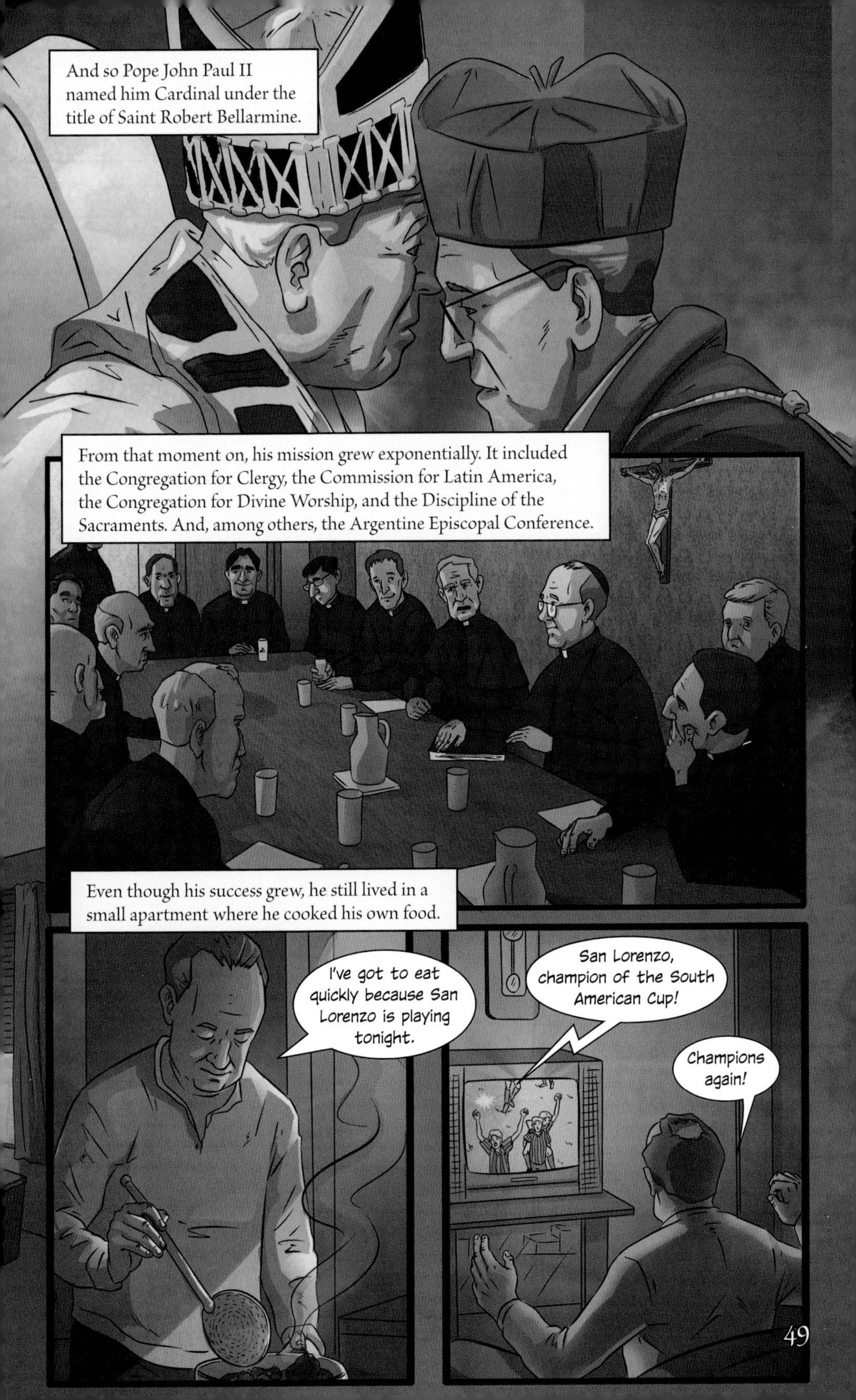
And so Pope John Paul II named him Cardinal under the title of Saint Robert Bellarmine.
From that moment on, his mission grew exponentially. It included the Congregation for Clergy, the Commission for Latin America, the Congregation for Divine Worship, and the Discipline of the Sacraments. And, among others, the Argentine Episcopal Conference.
Even though his success grew, he still lived in a small apartment where he cooked his own food.
I've got to eat quickly because San Lorenzo is playing tonight.
San Lorenzo, champion of the South American Cup!
Champions again!

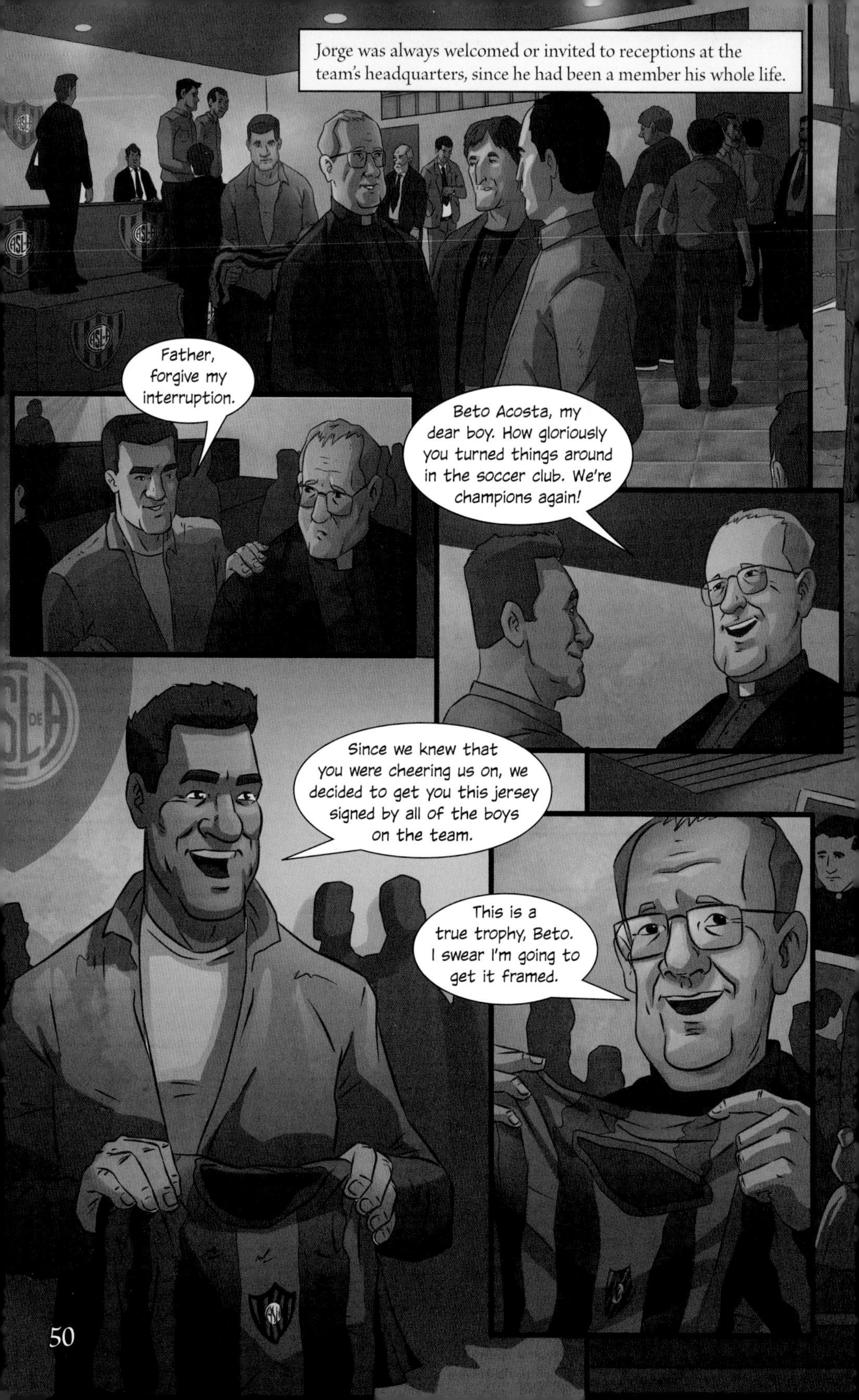
Jorge was always welcomed or invited to receptions at the team's headquarters, since he had been a member his whole life.
Father, forgive my interruption.
Beto Acosta, my dear boy. How gloriously you turned things around in the soccer club. We're champions again!
Since we knew that you were cheering us on, we decided to get you this jersey signed by all of the boys on the team.
This is a true trophy, Beto. I swear I'm going to get it framed.

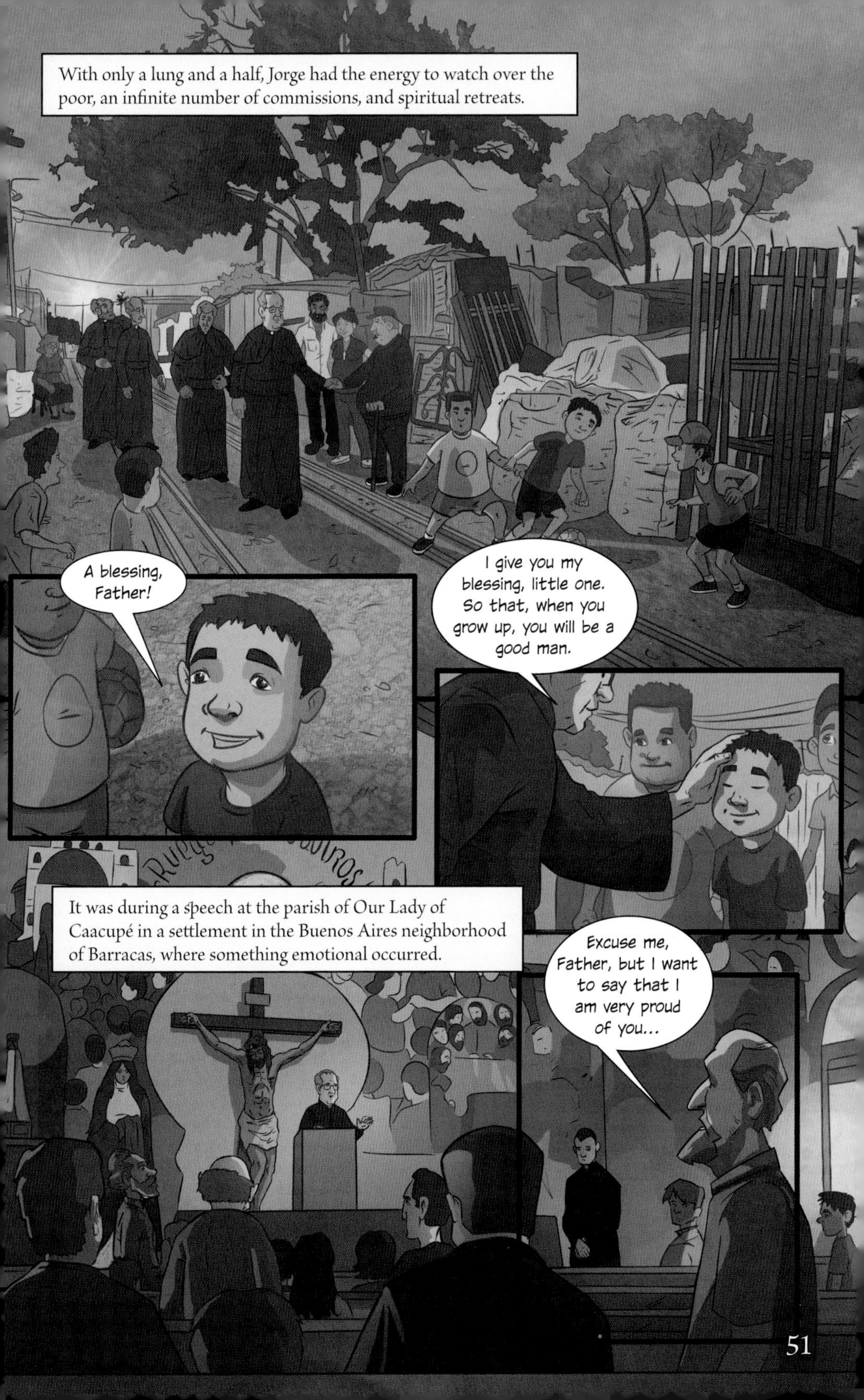
With only a lung and a half, Jorge had the energy to watch over the poor, an infinite number of commissions, and spiritual retreats.
A blessing, Father!
I give you my blessing, little one. So that, when you grow up, you will be a good man.
It was during a speech at the parish of Our Lady of Caacupé in a settlement in the Buenos Aires neighborhood of Barracas, where something emotional occurred.
Excuse me, Father, but I want to say that I am very proud of you...

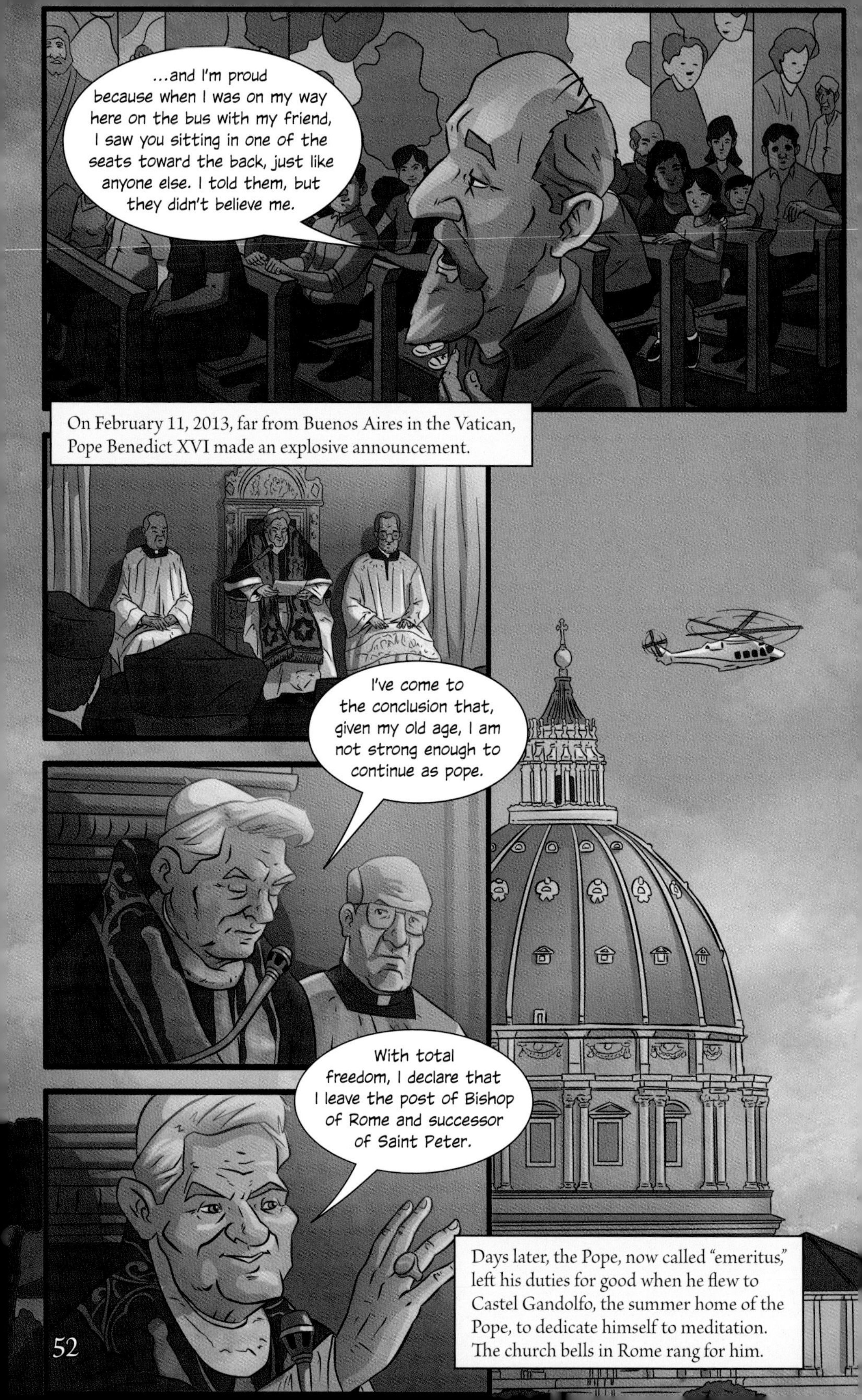
...and I'm proud because when I was on my way here on the bus with my friend, I saw you sitting in one of the seats toward the back, just like anyone else. I told them, but they didn't believe me.
On February 11, 2013, far from Buenos Aires in the Vatican, Pope Benedict XVI made an explosive announcement.
I've come to the conclusion that, given my old age, I am not strong enough to continue as pope.
With total freedom, I declare that I leave the post of Bishop of Rome and successor of Saint Peter.
Days later, the Pope, now called "emeritus," left his duties for good when he flew to Castel Gandolfo, the summer home of the Pope, to dedicate himself to meditation. The church bells in Rome rang for him.

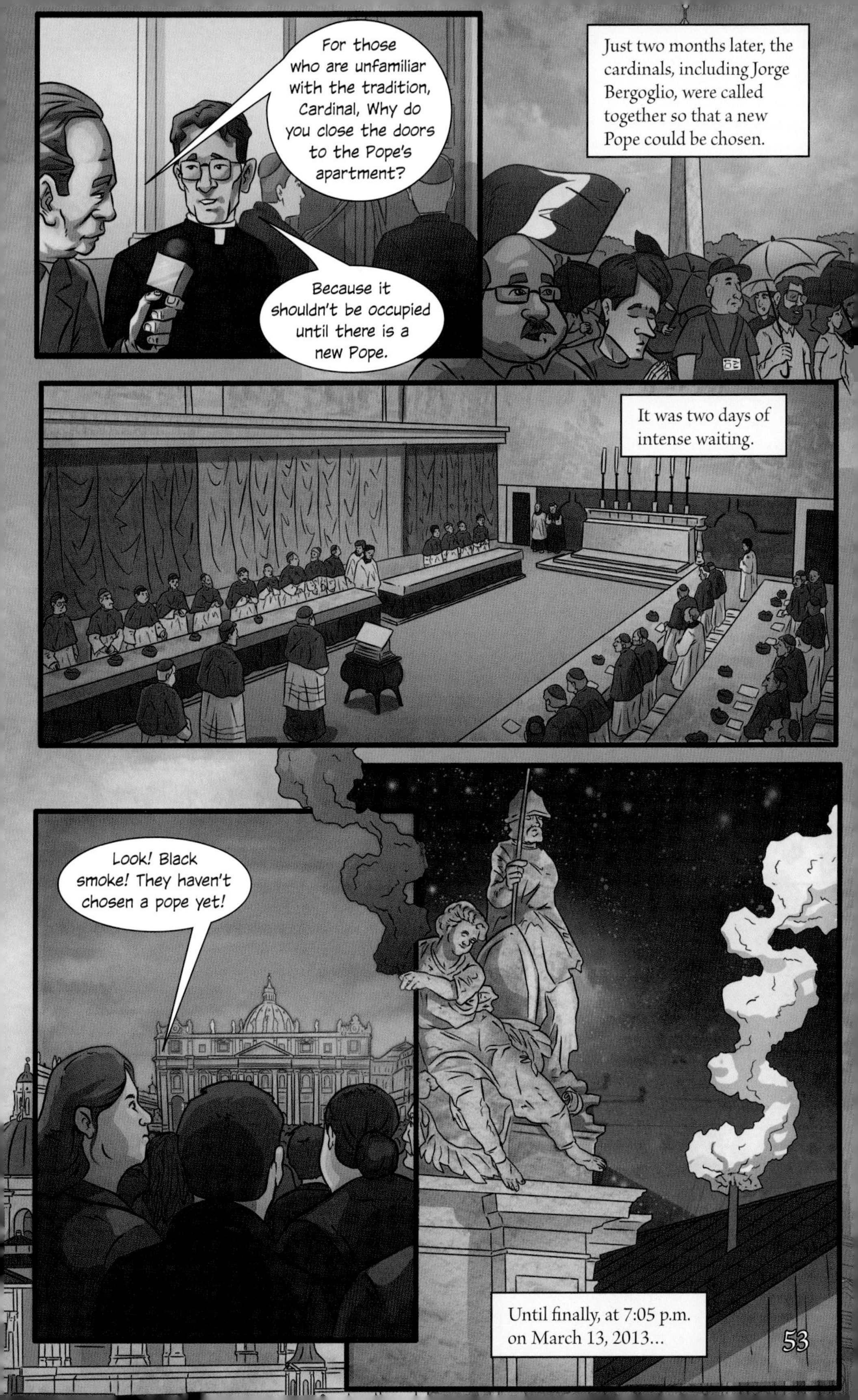
For those who are unfamiliar with the tradition, Cardinal, Why do you close the doors to the Pope's apartment?
Because it shouldn't be occupied until there is a new Pope.
Just two months later, the cardinals, including Jorge Bergoglio, were called together so that a new Pope could be chosen.
It was two days of intense waiting.
Look! Black smoke! They haven't chosen a pope yet!
Until finally, at 7:05 p.m. on March 13, 2013...

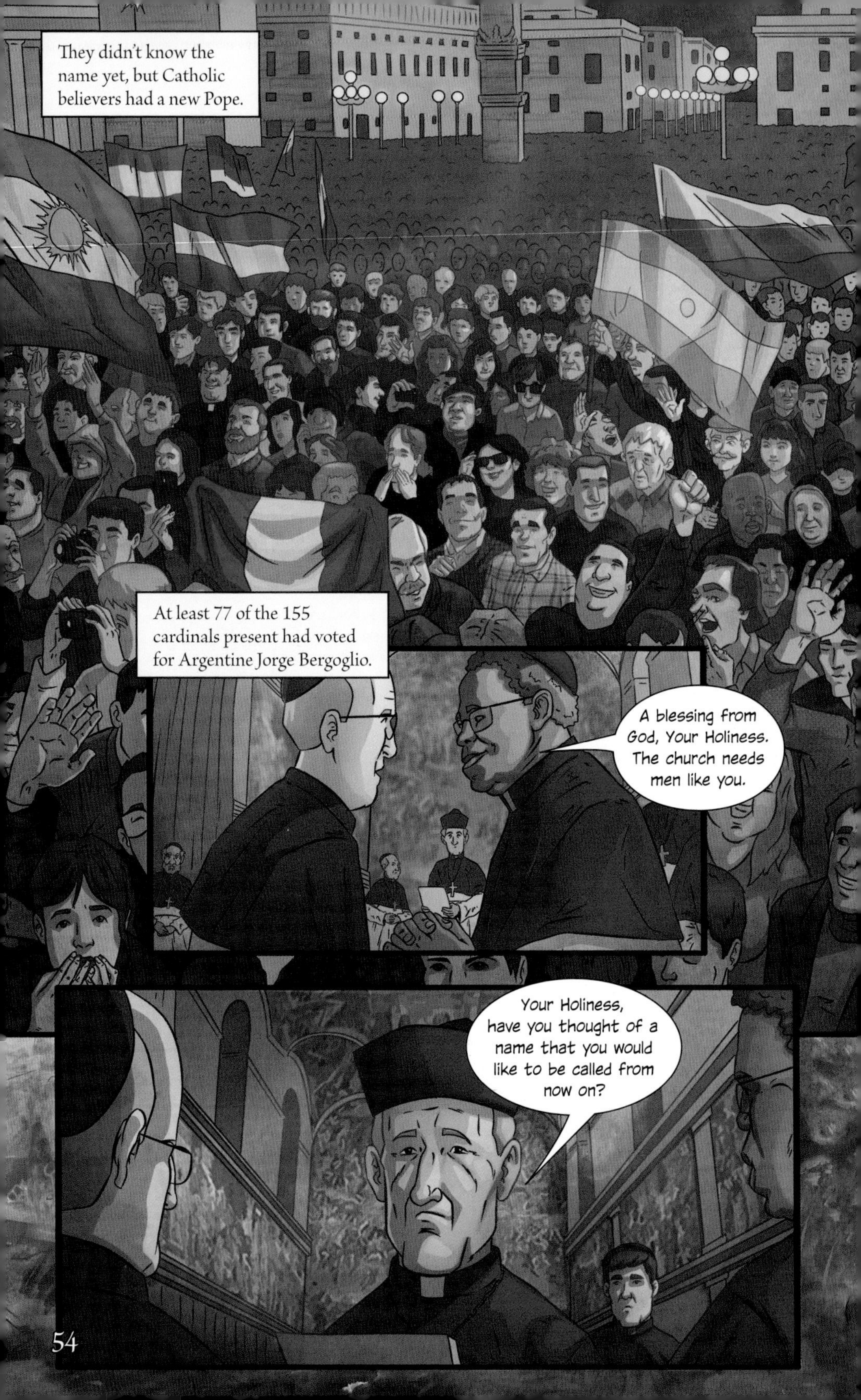
They didn't know the name yet, but Catholic believers had a new Pope.
At least 77 of the 155 cardinals present had voted for Argentine Jorge Bergoglio.
A blessing from God, Your Holiness. The church needs men like you.
Your Holiness, have you thought of a name that you would like to be called from now on?

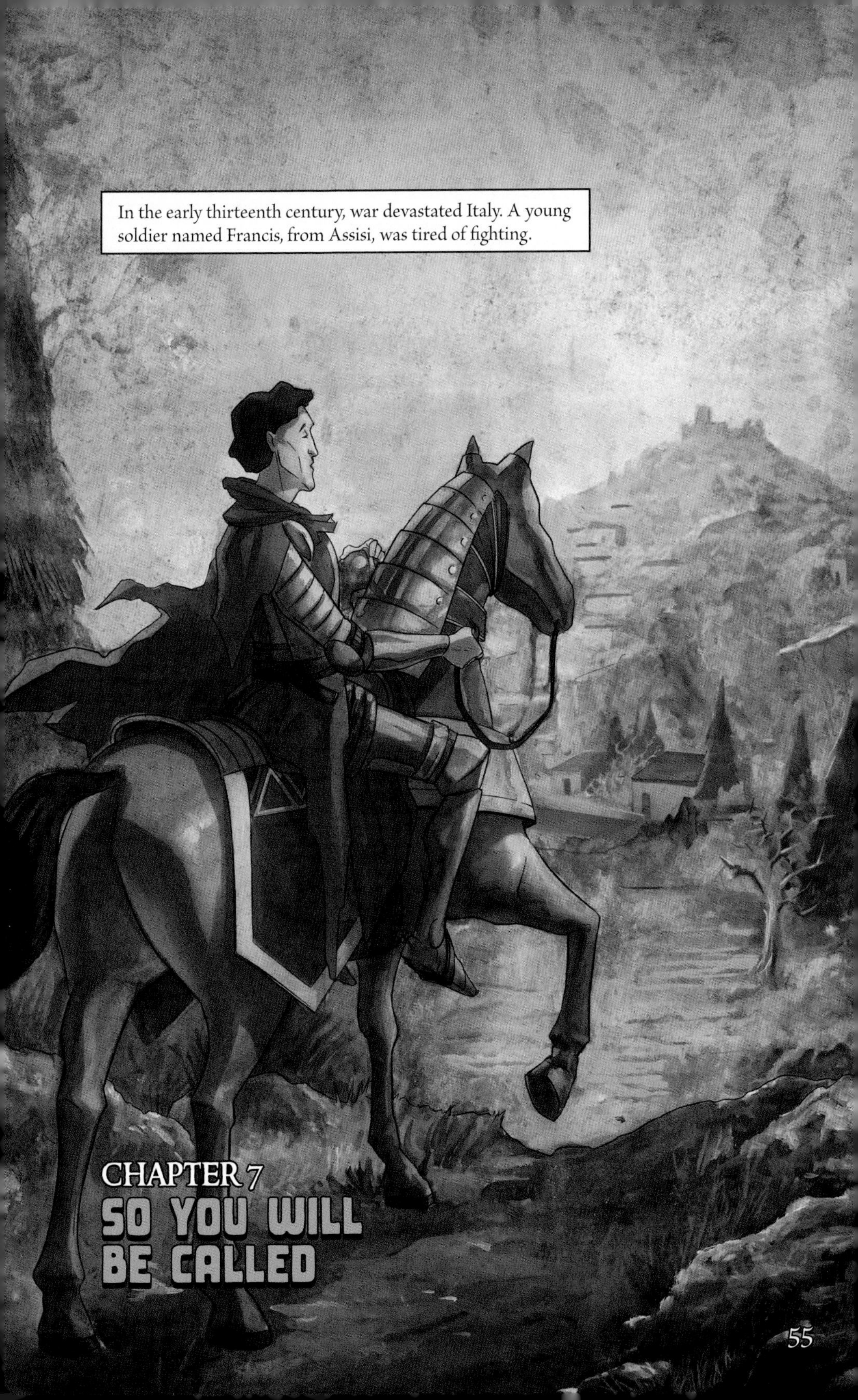
In the early thirteenth century, war devastated Italy. A young soldier named Francis, from Assisi, was tired of fighting.
CHAPTER 7
SO YOU WILL BE CALLED

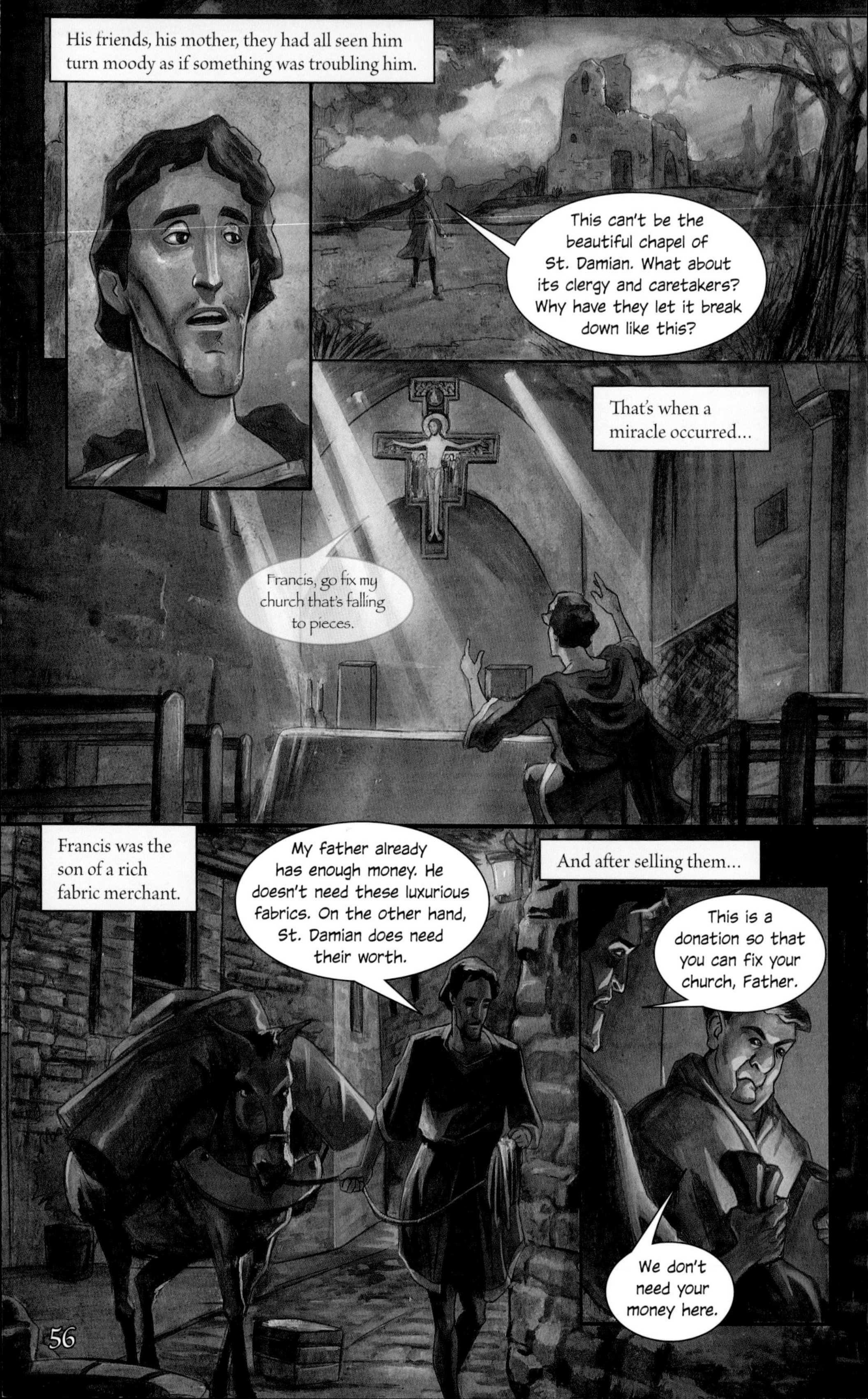

His friends, his mother, they had all seen him turn moody as if something was troubling him.
This can't be the beautiful chapel of St. Damian. What about its clergy and caretakers? Why have they let it break down like this?
That's when a miracle occurred...
Francis, go fix my church that's falling to pieces.
Francis was the son of a rich fabric merchant.
My father already has enough money. He doesn't need these luxurious fabrics. On the other hand, St. Damian does need their worth.
And after selling them...
This is a donation so that you can fix your church, Father.
We don't need your money here.

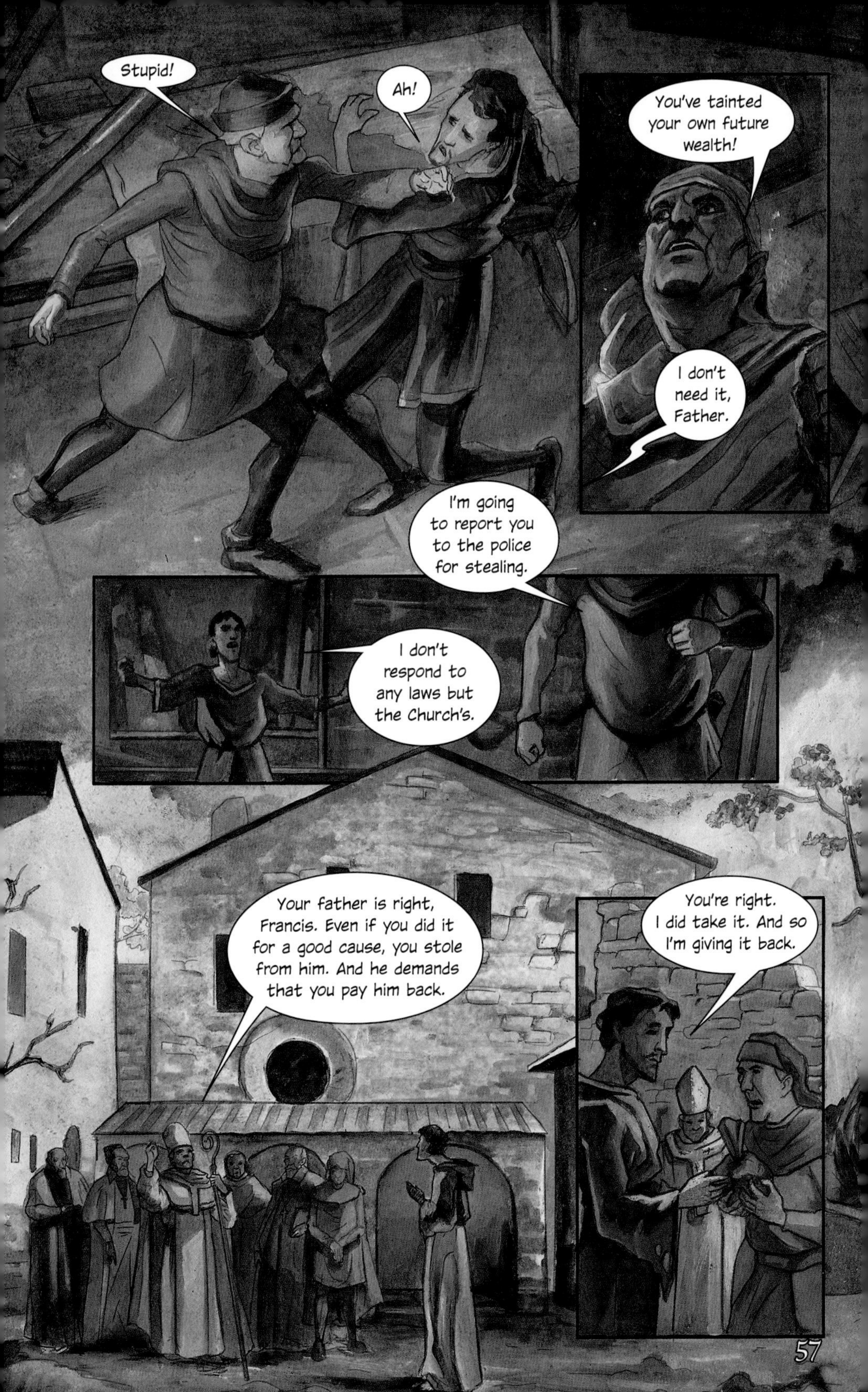
Stupid!
Ah!
You've tainted your own future wealth!
I don't need it, Father.
I'm going to report you to the police for stealing.
I don't respond to any laws but the Church's.
Your father is right, Francis. Even if you did it for a good cause, you stole from him. And he demands that you pay him back.
You're right. I did take it. And so I'm giving it back.

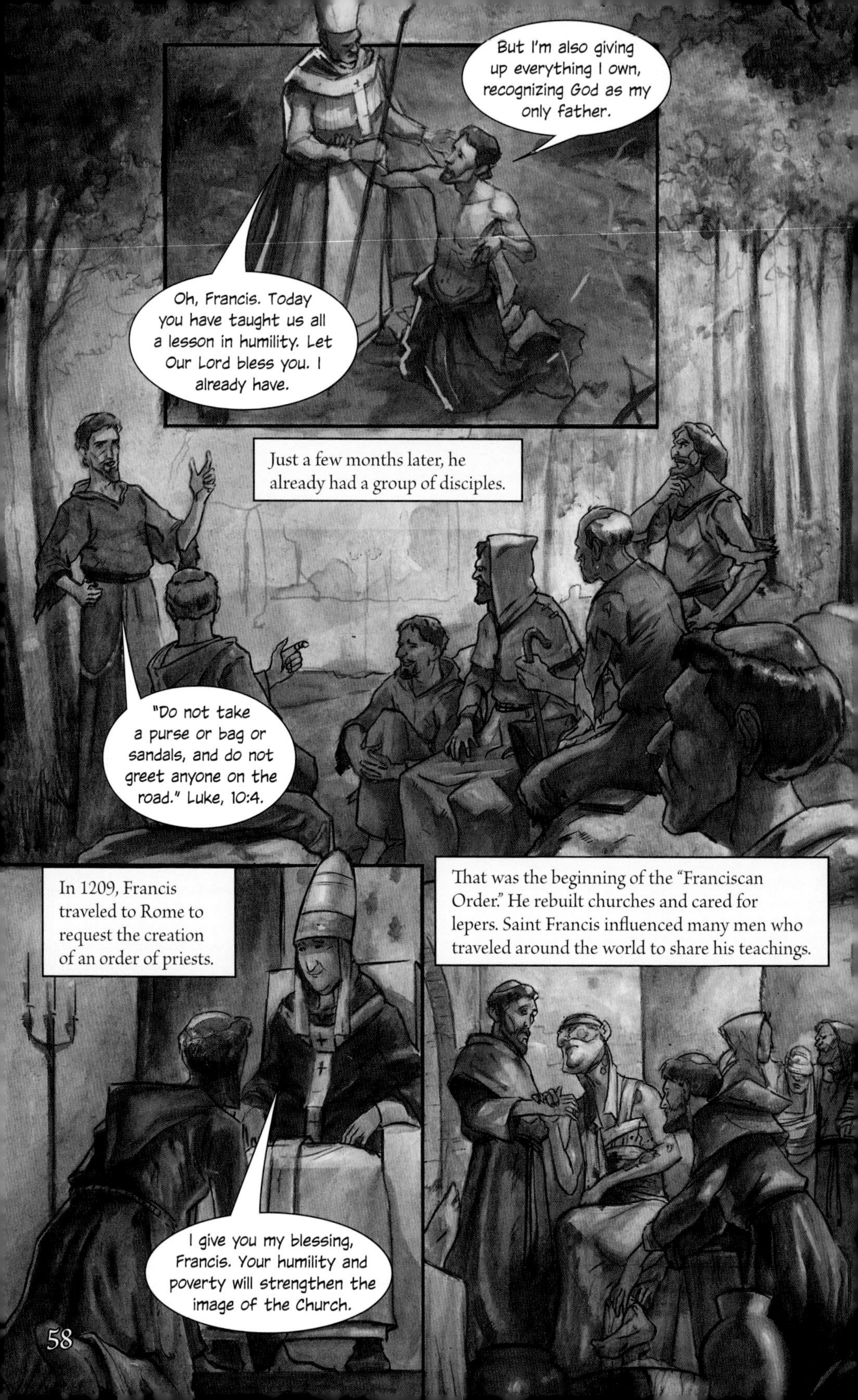
But I'm also giving up everything I own, recognizing God as my only father.
Oh, Francis. Today you have taught us all a lesson in humility. Let Our Lord bless you. I already have.
Just a few months later, he already had a group of disciples.
"Do not take a purse or bag or sandals, and do not greet anyone on the road." Luke, 10:4.
In 1209, Francis traveled to Rome to request the creation of an order of priests.
I give you my blessing, Francis. Your humility and poverty will strengthen the image of the Church.
That was the beginning of the "Franciscan Order." He rebuilt churches and cared for lepers. Saint Francis influenced many men who traveled around the world to share his teachings.

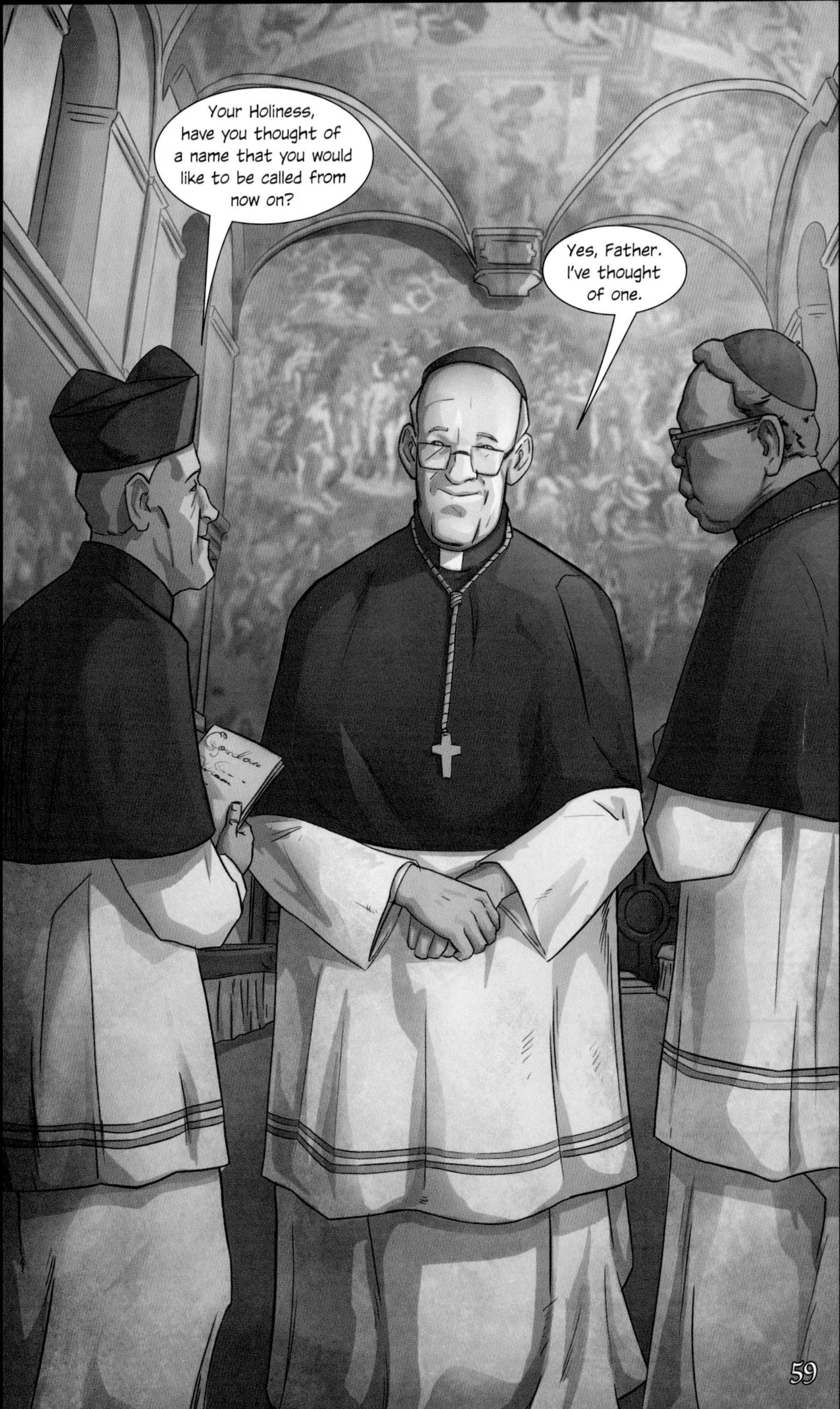
Your Holiness, have you thought of a name that you would like to be called from now on?
Yes, Father. I've thought of one.

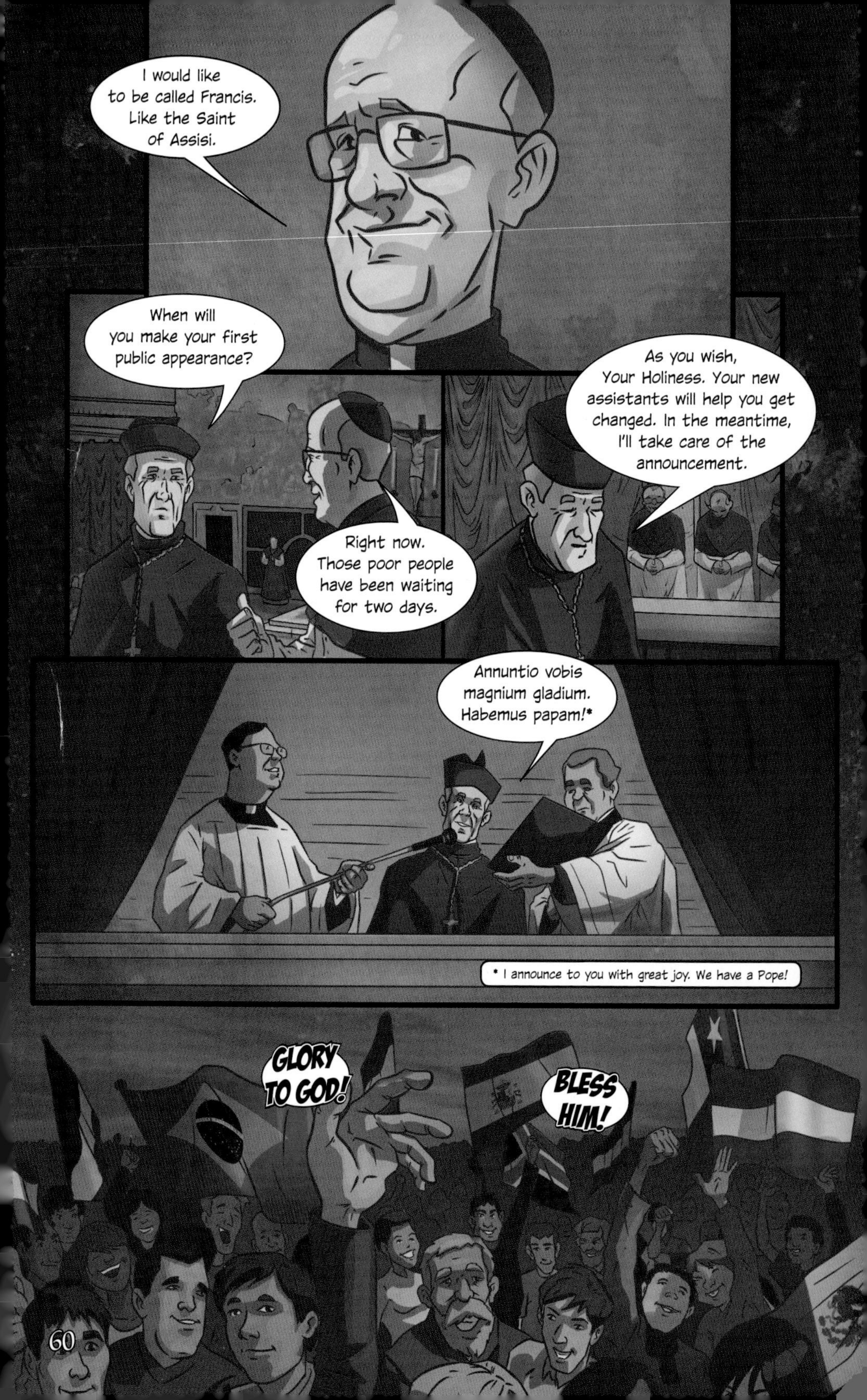
I would like to be called Francis. Like the Saint of Assisi.
When will you make your first public appearance?
Right now. Those poor people have been waiting for two days.
As you wish, Your Holiness. Your new assistants will help you get changed. In the meantime, I'll take care of the announcement.
Annuntio vobis magnium gladium. Habemus papam!*
* I announce to you with great joy. We have a Pope!
GLORY TO GOD!
BLESS HIM!

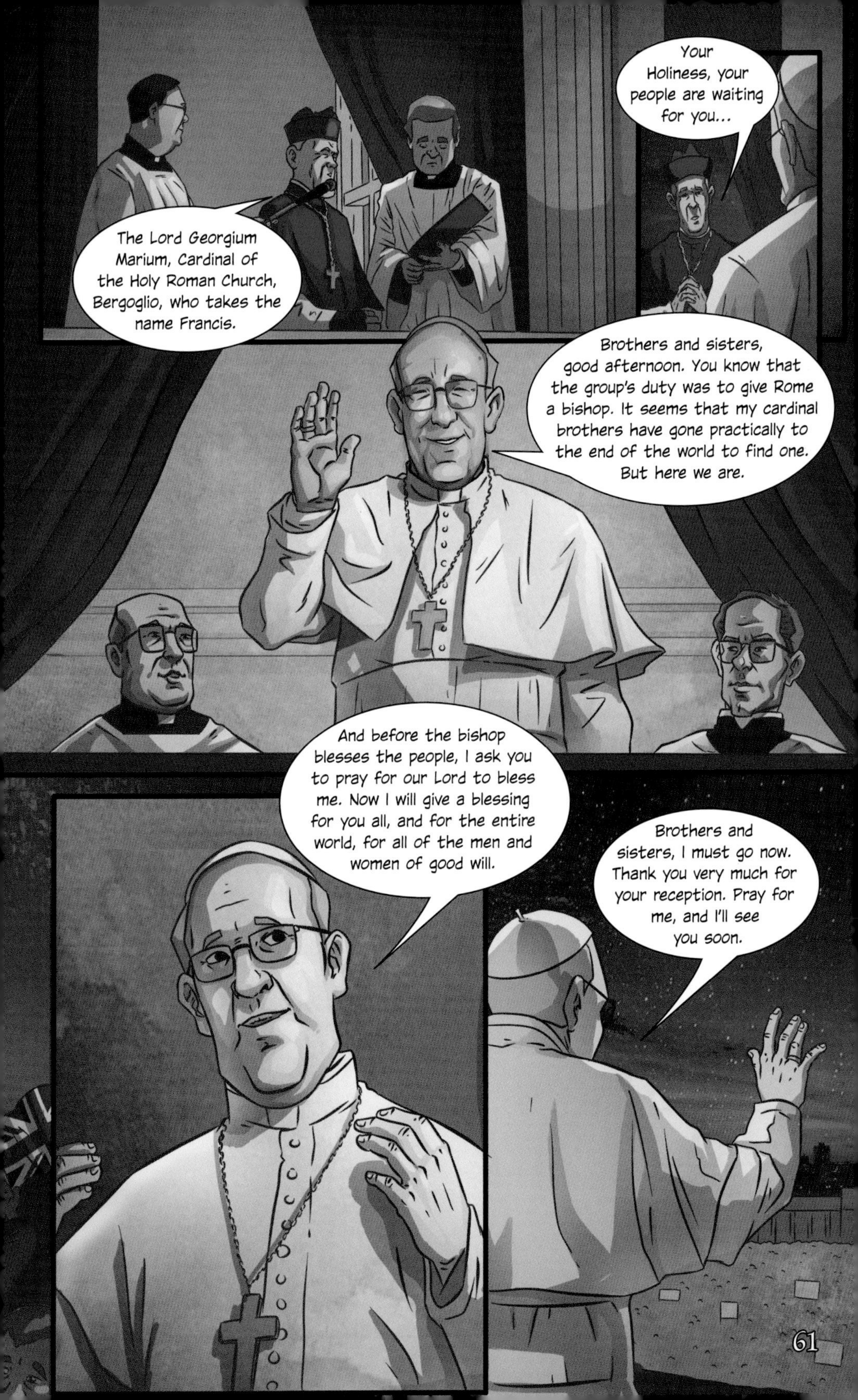

Your Holiness, your people are waiting for you...
The Lord Georgium Marium, Cardinal of the Holy Roman Church, Bergoglio, who takes the name Francis.
Brothers and sisters, good afternoon. You know that the group's duty was to give Rome a bishop. It seems that my cardinal brothers have gone practically to the end of the world to find one. But here we are.
And before the bishop blesses the people, I ask you to pray for our Lord to bless me. Now I will give a blessing for you all, and for the entire world, for all of the men and women of good will.
Brothers and sisters, I must go now. Thank you very much for your reception. Pray for me, and I'll see you soon.

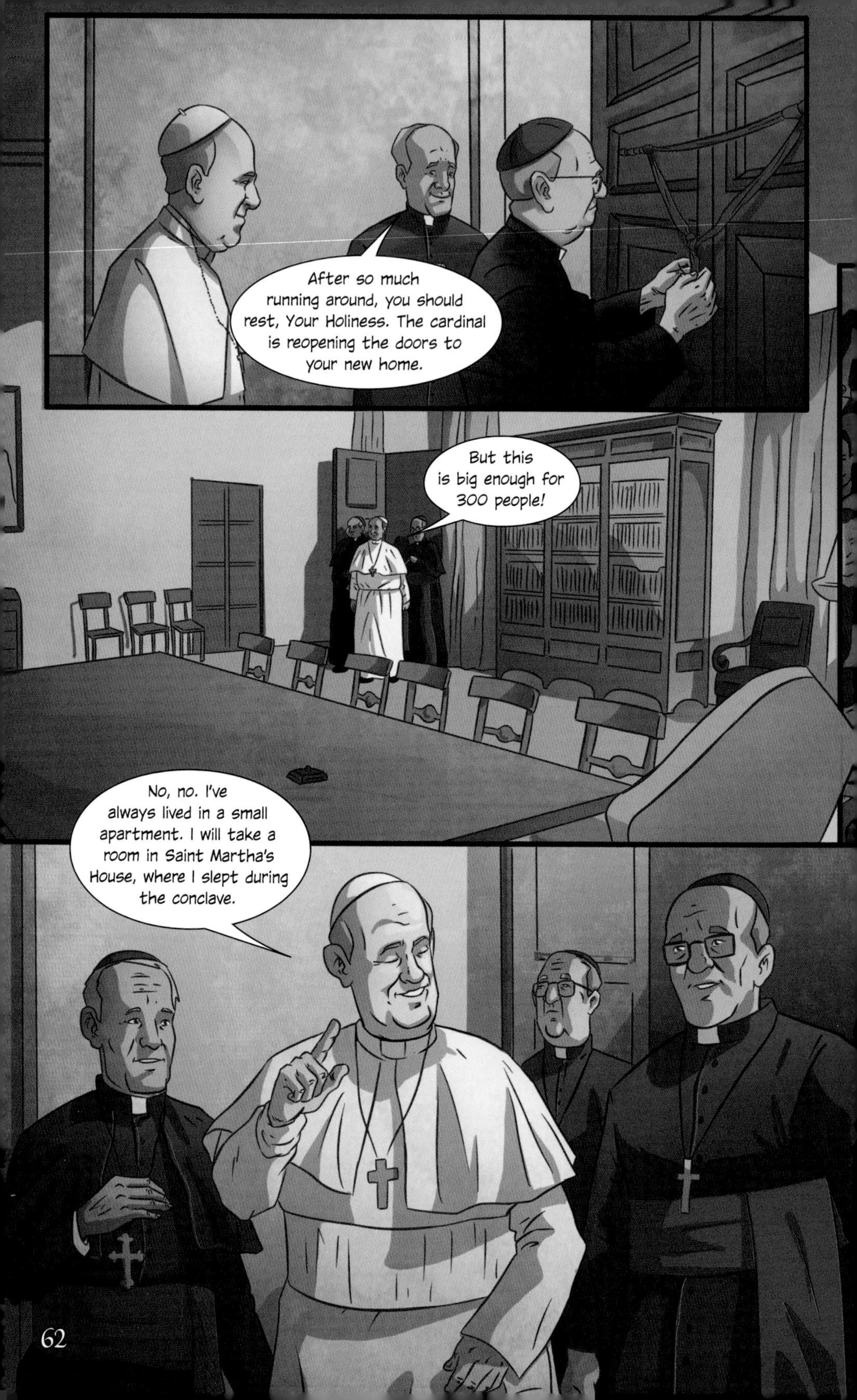
After so much running around, you should rest, Your Holiness. The cardinal is reopening the doors to your new home.
But this is big enough for 300 people!
No, no. I've always lived in a small apartment. I will take a room in Saint Martha's House, where I slept during the conclave.

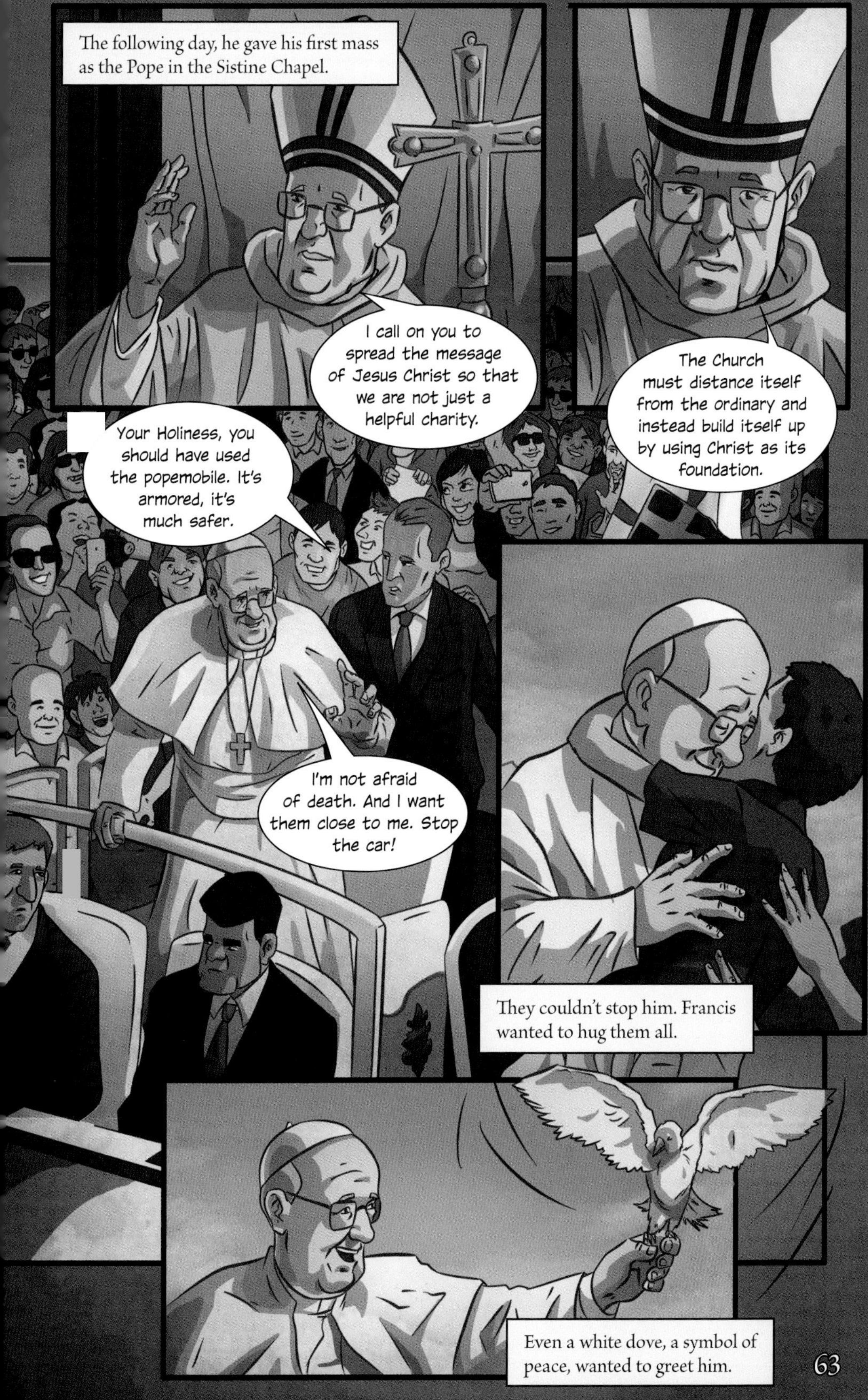
The following day, he gave his first mass as the Pope in the Sistine Chapel.
I call on you to spread the message of Jesus Christ so that we are not just a helpful charity.
The Church must distance itself from the ordinary and instead build itself up by using Christ as its foundation.
Your Holiness, you should have used the popemobile. It's armored, it's much safer.
I'm not afraid of death. And I want them close to me. Stop the car!
They couldn't stop him. Francis wanted to hug them all.
Even a white dove, a symbol of peace, wanted to greet him.

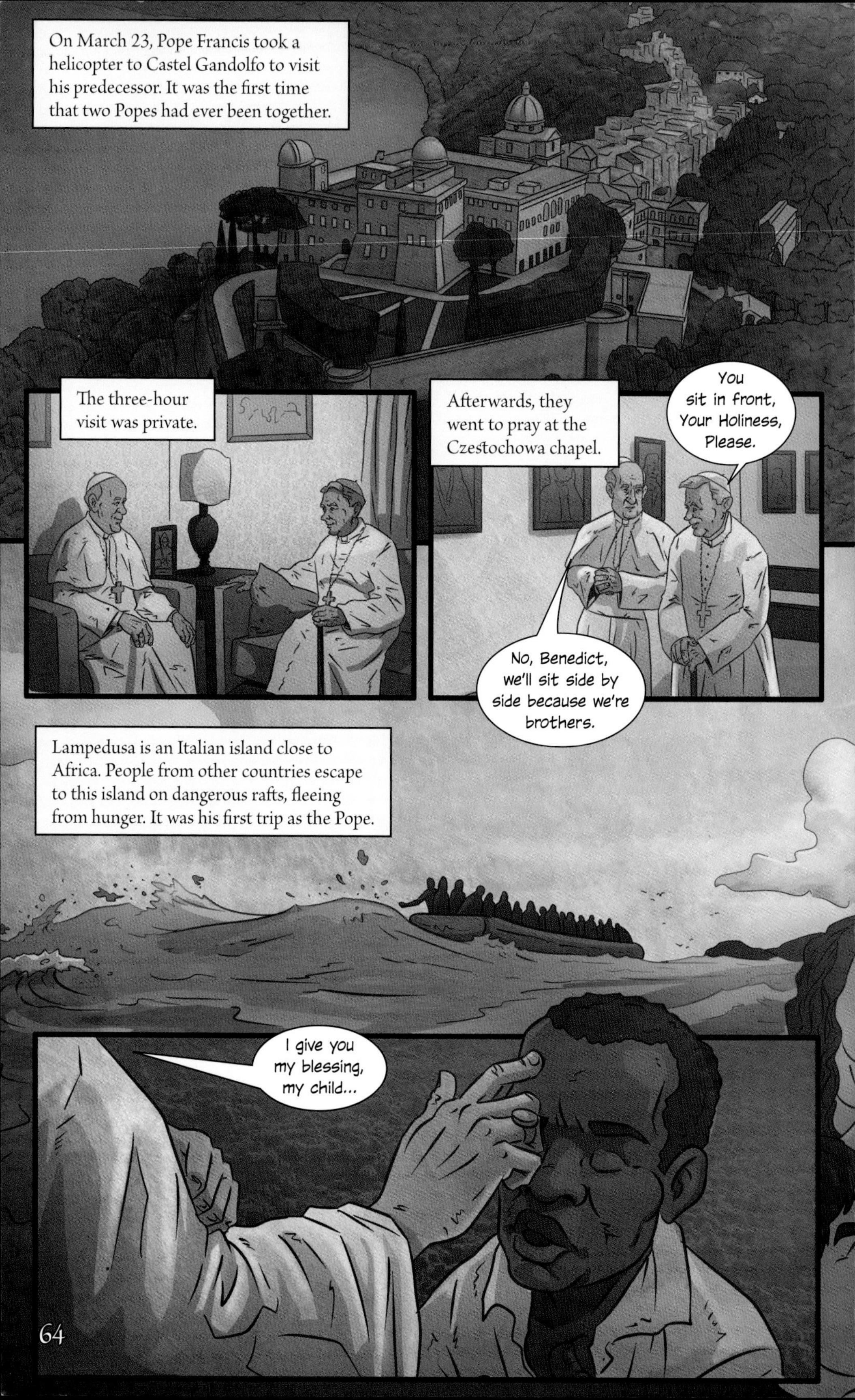

On March 23, Pope Francis took a helicopter to Castel Gandolfo to visit his predecessor. It was the first time that two Popes had ever been together.
The three-hour visit was private.
Afterwards, they went to pray at the Częstochowa chapel.
You sit in front, Your Holiness, Please.
No, Benedict, we'll sit side by side because we're brothers.
Lampedusa is an Italian island close to Africa. People from other countries escape to this island on dangerous rafts, fleeing from hunger. It was his first trip as the Pope.
I give you my blessing, my child...

From July 22 to 29, 2013, Pope Francis attended the World Youth Days in Río de Janeiro, Brazil.

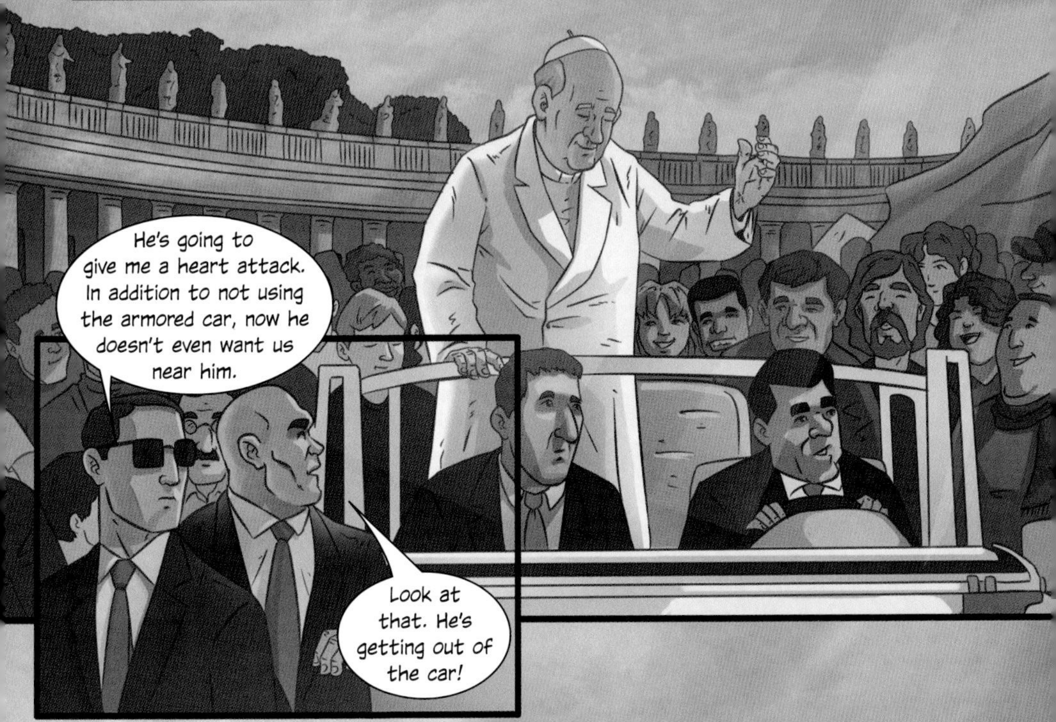
He's going to give me a heart attack. In addition to not using the armored car, now he doesn't even want us near him.
Look at that. He's getting out of the car!

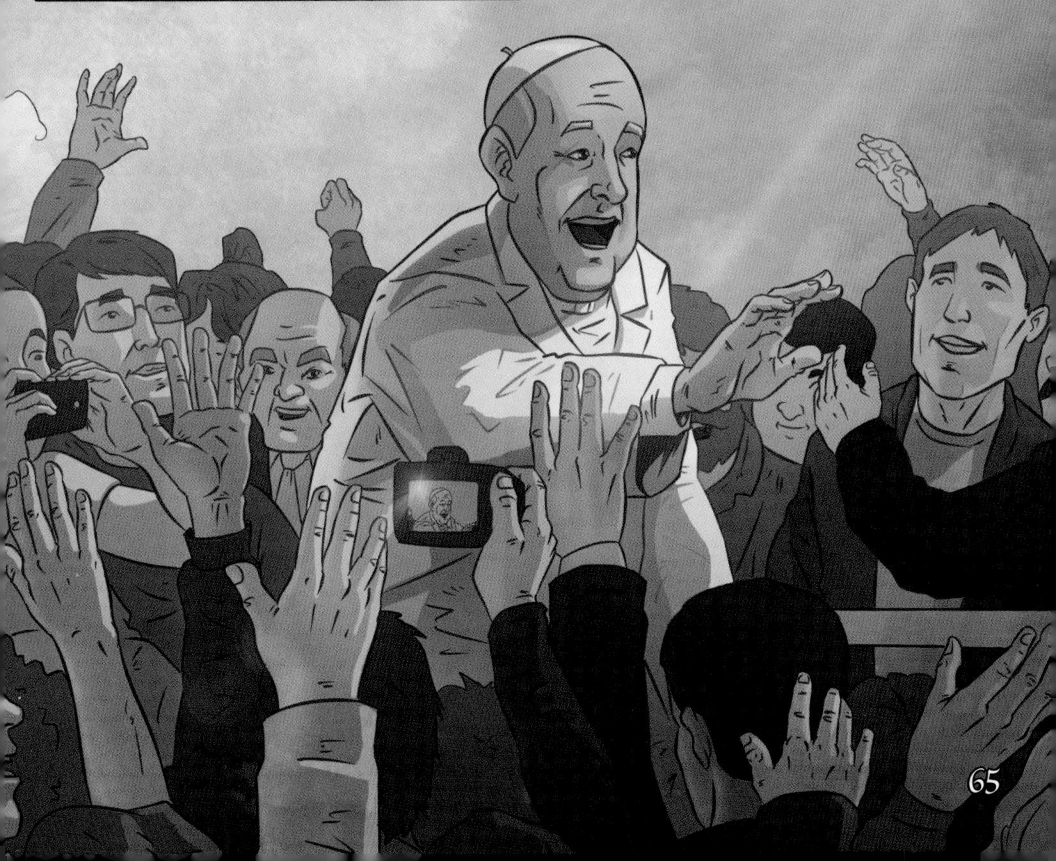

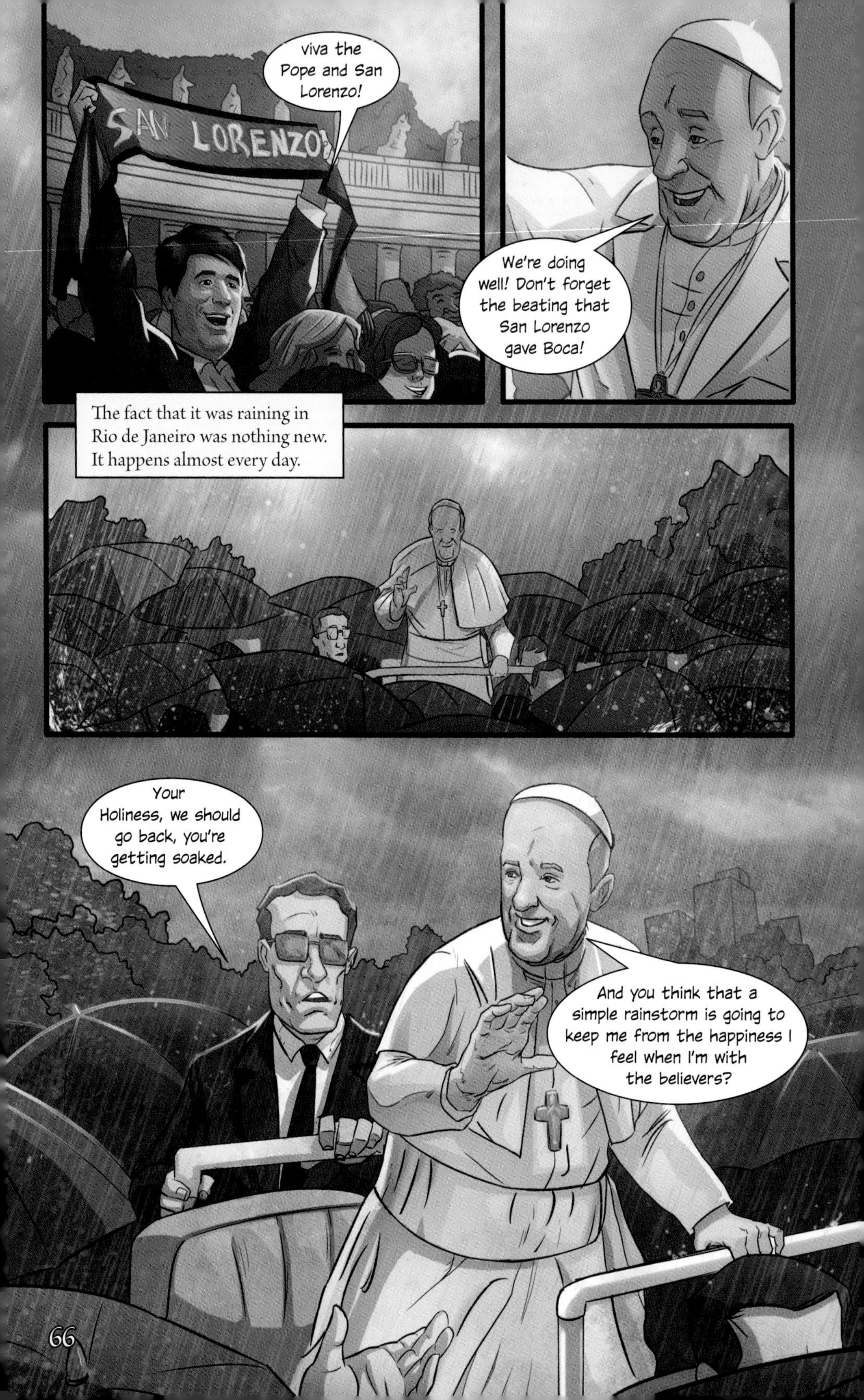
SAN LORENZO
viva the Pope and San Lorenzo!
We're doing well! Don't forget the beating that San Lorenzo gave Boca!
The fact that it was raining in Rio de Janeiro was nothing new. It happens almost every day.
Your Holiness, we should go back, you're getting soaked.
And you think that a simple rainstorm is going to keep me from the happiness I feel when I'm with the believers?

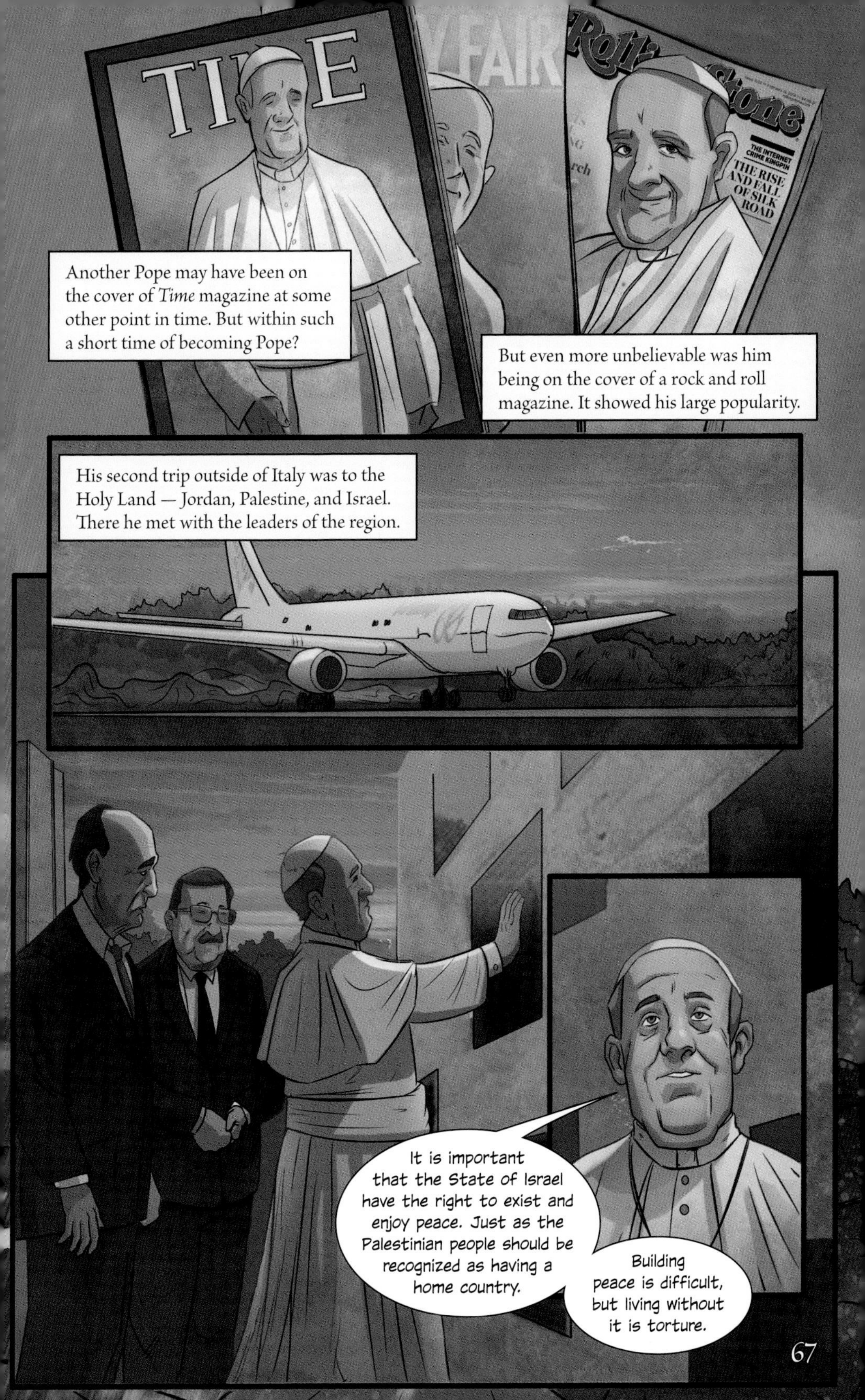
TIME
THE INTERNET CRIME KINGPIN
THE RISE AND FALL OF SILK ROAD
Another Pope may have been on the cover of *Time* magazine at some other point in time. But within such a short time of becoming Pope?
But even more unbelievable was him being on the cover of a rock and roll magazine. It showed his large popularity.
His second trip outside of Italy was to the Holy Land — Jordan, Palestine, and Israel. There he met with the leaders of the region.
It is important that the State of Israel have the right to exist and enjoy peace. Just as the Palestinian people should be recognized as having a home country.
Building peace is difficult, but living without it is torture.

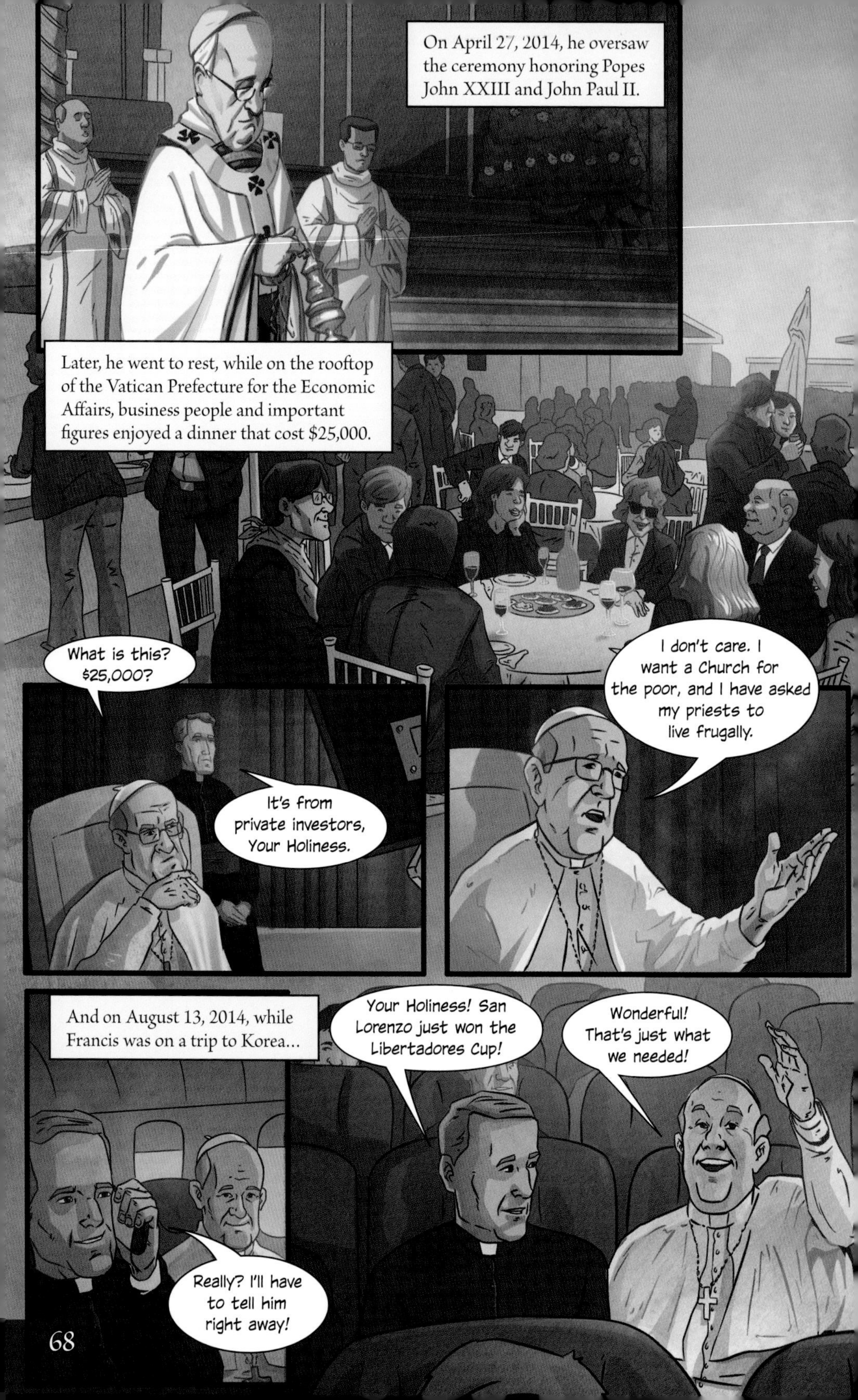
On April 27, 2014, he oversaw the ceremony honoring Popes John XXIII and John Paul II.
Later, he went to rest, while on the rooftop of the Vatican Prefecture for the Economic Affairs, business people and important figures enjoyed a dinner that cost $25,000.
What is this? $25,000?
It's from private investors, Your Holiness.
I don't care. I want a Church for the poor, and I have asked my priests to live frugally.
And on August 13, 2014, while Francis was on a trip to Korea...
Really? I'll have to tell him right away!
Your Holiness! San Lorenzo just won the Libertadores Cup!
Wonderful! That's just what we needed!

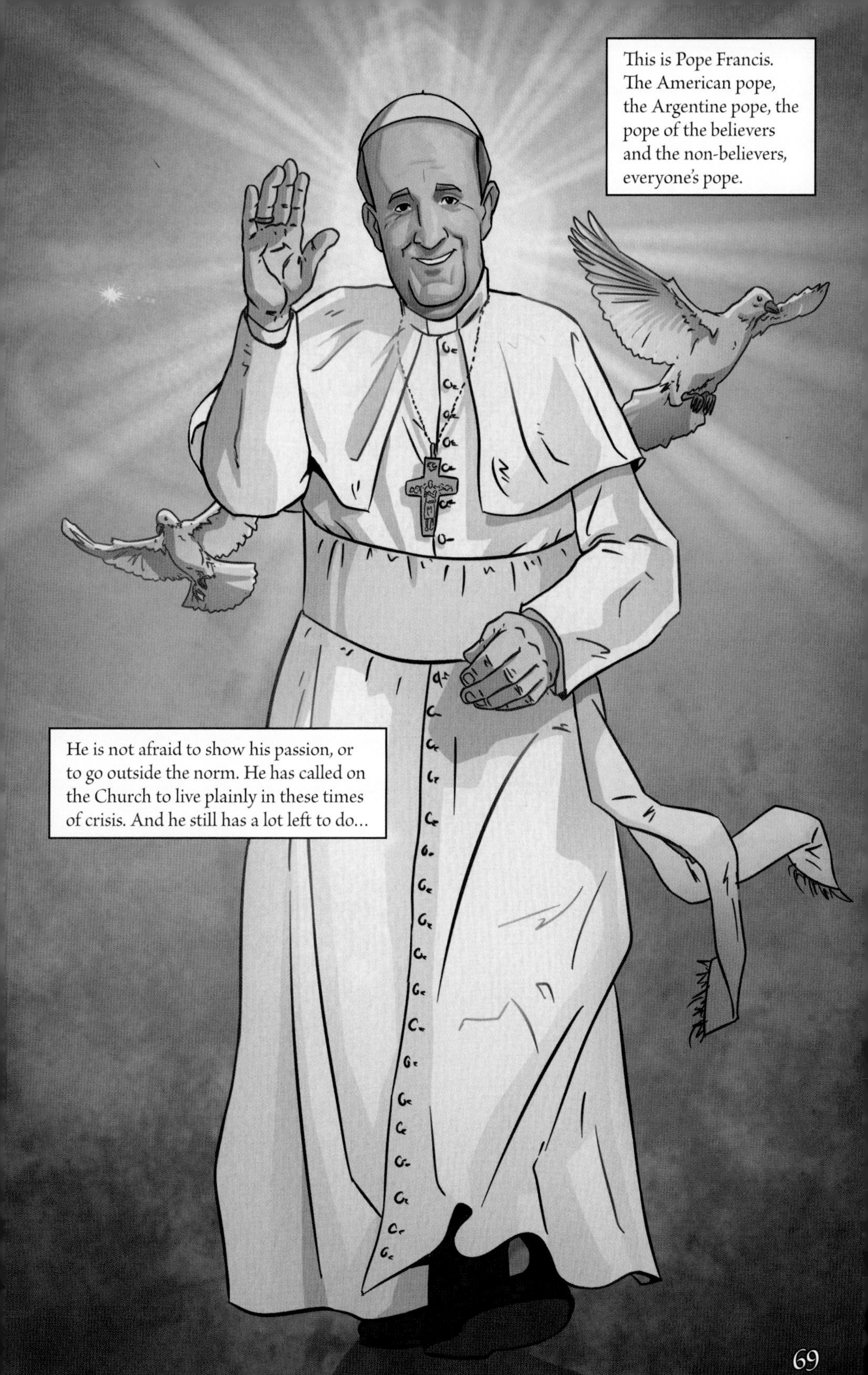
This is Pope Francis. The American pope, the Argentine pope, the pope of the believers and the non-believers, everyone's pope.
He is not afraid to show his passion, or to go outside the norm. He has called on the Church to live plainly in these times of crisis. And he still has a lot left to do…

TIMELINE
1936-PRESENT

1936	1940	1950	1960	1970
Jorge Bergoglio was born on December 17 in Buenos Aires. He was baptized at the Basilica of San Carlos Borromeo and María Auxiliadora, which belongs to the Salesian congregation.	Bergoglio spent his childhood in the Buenos Aires neighborhood of Flores with a typical, large family of Italian immigrants. He got his love of art from his mother and his love of the San Lorenzo soccer club of Almagro from his father. When he was 13 years old, he finished elementary school and got his first job at a sock factory, where he worked as a cleaner.	Bergoglio did his high school studies at a school that specialized in chemistry. When he was 17 years old, he began working in a laboratory. One year later, he finished high school. At the age of 20, he started seminary with the goal of becoming a priest. When he was 21 years old, he suffered a severe case of pneumonia that almost killed him and required the removal of a part of his lung.	In Seminary, Bergoglio studied classic sciences, deepening his knowledge of history, literature, Latin, and Greek. From 1964 to 1966, he taught literature and psychology. On December 13, 1969, on the cusp of turning 33 years old, he was ordained as a priest.	In 1973, Bergoglio was named Provincial Superior of the Argentine Jesuits (the order that he belongs to), a post that he would hold until 1979. During the most recent military dictatorship in Argentina (1976-1983), he helped priests who were persecuted for their work in poor communities.

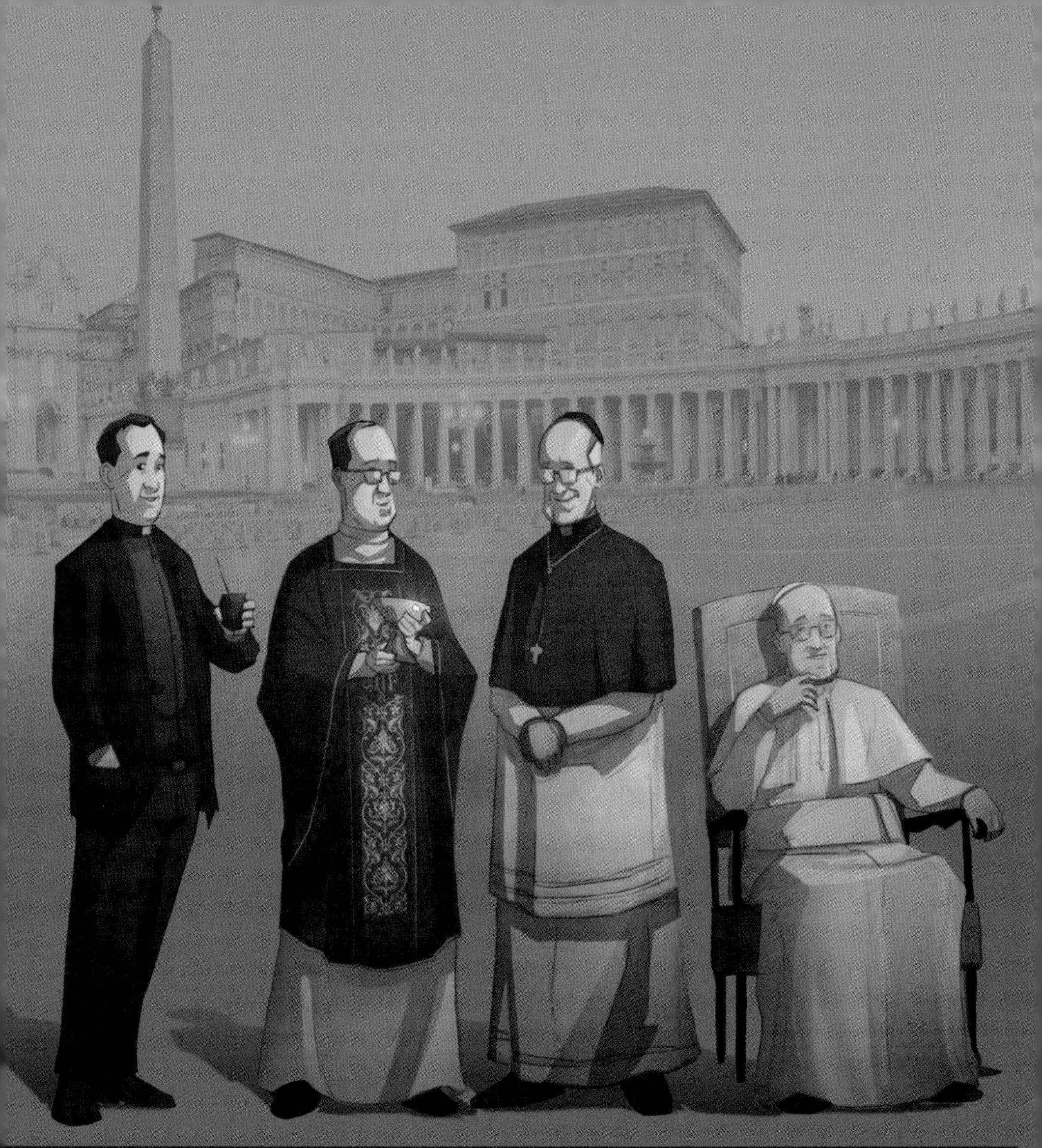

1980	1990	2000	2010
From 1980 to 1986, Bergoglio acted as Rector of the Colegio Máximo de San Miguel in its schools of philosophy and theology. In 1986, he traveled to Germany to complete his doctoral thesis. He later returned to work in the El Salvador school in Buenos Aires.	In 1992, Bergoglio was named Auxiliary Bishop of Buenos Aires. In 1998, after the death of Cardinal Antonio Quarracino, he became Archbishop of Buenos Aires, the most important position in the Argentine Church.	In 2001, Bergoglio was named Cardinal by then Pope John Paul II. During this decade, he acted as Archbishop of Buenos Aires, demonstrating his humility and frugality day after day. He was also committed to important campaigns against drugs and human trafficking. In 2005, after the death of John Paul II, he came in second in the conclave that chose Benedict XVI as his successor.	In February 2013, Benedict XVI announced his resignation as Pope. On March 13 of that same year, Bergoglio was chosen to be the successor of Benedict XVI, the first Latin American and Jesuit Pope. Francis currently represents a possible reorganization of the Church, pushing it closer to the poorest and neediest members of society.

WHO IS FRANCIS?

Pope Francis is the first ever Latin American Pope, and the first non-European since the year 741. He is also the first Pope to belong to the Society of Jesus. Because of this, and because of his constant gestures and dedication to the neediest people in the world, his role as Pope is considered to be a new and exciting step.

Jorge Bergoglio was born on December 17, 1936, in Buenos Aires, the son of Regina María Sívori, a housewife, and Mario José Bergoglio, a railroad employee. Jorge grew up in the Flores neighborhood, in a family of Italian immigrants who had arrived in Argentina in search of a more prosperous future. Following that search, Jorge's parents focused on getting him a good education, as he was the oldest of five children. Given their efforts, he was able to earn the high school title of chemical technician.

The scientific nature of his studies did not keep young Jorge from responding to God's calling. So he prepared to become a priest. He started seminary at the age of 20; two years later, he joined the Society of Jesus. In 1969, after ten years of intense study, he became an ordained priest.

After acting as a teacher and priest for many years, he became the Auxiliary Bishop of Buenos Aires. And after the death of Archbishop Quarracino, he came to hold the most important post in the Argentine Church: Archbishop of Buenos Aires and Primate of Argentina. In 2001, he was named Cardinal, and in March 2013, he was elected and named Pope, under the name of Francis.

Despite all of the important positions that he held and continues to hold, he was never blinded by power, nor did he lose sight of his commitment to the poor and the fight for social justice.

FRANCIS AND THE MOVIES

Despite the fact that Francis has only been a world-renowned figure for a few years, there are already a few movies with him as the main character. They are mainly documentaries that narrate his life and role as Pope. But in 2016, an Argentine biographical miniseries launched, called Call Me Francis. The story centers on the last military dictatorship in Argentina and Jorge Bergoglio's efforts to help priests persecuted by the government.

The figure of Saint Francis of Assisi has also been portrayed in movies. For example, the classic movie Brother Sun, Sister Moon, a 1972 British-Italian co-production, dramatizes the life of this poor saint. Major parts of this movie were filmed in the town of Assisi.

The work of the Jesuits in America was also the subject of a 1986 movie, The Mission. It features renowned actors Robert de Niro and Jeremy Irons. This film tells the story of an eighteenth century Jesuit missionary's efforts to protect a group of native people living in an evangelized community from the Portuguese army. The movie is set in the impressive Amazon jungle and the Iguazú Falls.

HIS THREE INSPIRATIONS

Francis is known for his very diverse education. His specialized high school studies in chemistry blended well with his study of humanities, literature, philosophy, and theology, as he studied to become a priest. Similarly, his religious training was also inspired by a number of fields, contributing to his unique personality as Pope.

Saint John Bosco

Francis was baptized as Jorge Bergoglio at the Basilica of San Carlos Borromeo and María Auxiliadora in Buenos Aires. The church was an important hub for the Salesian congregation in Argentina. This congregation was founded by Saint John Bosco (1815–1888) around 1859 in Turin, Italy, and is known for its work with young people, especially those who are poor.

As a young priest from a modest upbringing, Saint John Bosco was able to understand the needs of his time. He made it his goal to gather children who lived on the street and teach them trades that would allow them to make a living for themselves. He also brought communities together to educate them on Christian values. At first, the young priest was considered crazy. But over time, his work was recognized for how it improved the lives of the poor populations. The Salesian project would soon expand to the rest of the world, and Argentina was the first country outside of Europe where it arrived.

Ignatius of Loyola

Francis is the first Pope from the religious order called the Society of Jesus, whose members are commonly known as "Jesuits." It was founded in 1534 by Ignatius of Loyola (1491–1556). Loyola was a Spanish military man who, after being injured in combat, rediscovered his Catholic faith by reading religious texts. From that moment on, he left his weapons behind and set out for forgiveness for his past life. At the Monastery of Montserrat in Barcelona, he hung his armor in front of the image of the Virgin Mary. He left dressed in rags to continue his pilgrimage. He finally settled in as a hermit in a cave in Manresa. He used this experience to write his book, Spiritual Exercises, which would become the foundation for the Society of Jesus.

This order is made up of priests who carry out spiritual, social, and educational activities, mostly for the poor. When joining this order, priests take three vows to be poor, celibate, and obedient, in tune with Jesus' poor and humble lifestyle. In Latin America, the Jesuits carried out important missionary work among the indigenous people there and also founded schools and universities.

Saint Francis of Assisi

On March 13, 2013, Father Jorge became known around the world as Francis. He is the first Pope to take the name of the poor saint from Assisi, the founder of the Franciscan order, or "the order of friars minor."

Francis of Assisi (1182–1226) was the son of a rich merchant in his city and a noblewoman. In 1202, he became involved in a war between Assisi and Perugia, leading him to spend some time in captivity. From that moment on, he began to feel unsatisfied with his lifestyle and decided to join the ministry to serve the poor. In 1206, he publicly declined his inheritance. He started preaching, with poverty as a fundamental value, and proposed a simple lifestyle based on the ideals of the Gospel.

The following phrase, popularly attributed to the saint from Assisi, helps to understand the life of Pope Francis: "My brothers, the Lord called me into the way of simplicity and humility, and this way He has pointed out to me for myself and for those who will believe and follow me..."

GLOSSARY

acolyte (ak-eh-LITE)—a person who assists a member of the clergy in a service

arrogant (A-ruh-guhnt)—conceited and too proud

baptize (BAP-tize)—to pour water on someone as part of a Christian religious practice

bishop (BI-shuhp)—a senior priest in the Catholic Church

catechism (CAT-eh-kism)—a summary of religious teachings in the form of questions and answers

chemistry (KEM-is-tree)—the scientific study of substances and their composition

clergy (KLUR-jee)—minister, priest, or other person appointed to carry out religious work

communion (kuh-MYOO-yun)—a Christian ceremony that honors Jesus' Last Supper, with clergy serving bread and wine

congregation (KAHN-grih-gay-shuhn)—people who meet for worship

dictatorship (DIK-tay-tuhr-ship)—a government ruled by someone who took complete control of a country; dictatorships are usually ruled unjustly

doctrine (DAWK-trin)—set of beliefs or rules

frugal (FROO-guhl)—someone who lives very carefully so as not to waste anything, especially money

humble (huhm-buhl)—not proud

leper (LEP-uhr)—used to described someone with a disease that attacks the nerves, skin and muscles

mission (MISH-uhn)—church or other place where people work on behalf of a religious group to spread the group's faith

modest (MOD-ist)—someone who is not boastful about his or her abilities, possessions, or achievements

ordination (or-dih-NAY-shuhn)—the act of making someone a Christian priest or minister through a special ceremony

pneumonia (noo-MOH-nyuh)—a serious disease that causes the lungs to become inflamed and filled with a thick fluid that makes breathing difficult

Pope (POHP)—the head of the Roman Catholic Church

progressive (pruh-GRESS-iv)—in favor of improvement, progress, and reform, especially in political or social matters

sacrament (SAK-rah-mehnt)—a holy rite in a Christian church, such as baptism, communion, or confession

sacred (SAY-krid)—holy or having to do with religion

sacrifice (SAK-ruh-fise)—to give up something important or enjoyable for a good reason; to offer something to a god

seminary (sem-ih-NAYR-ee)—school where students are trained to become ministers or priests

sexton (SEKS-ton)—an official of the church who takes care of church buildings and properties

DISCUSSION QUESTIONS

1. What lessons did Jorge learn from working at the laboratory? How do you think this influenced his life in the long run?

2. Why do you think it was hard for Jorge's mom to accept his decision to become a priest? Have you ever been afraid to tell your parents something because of how they would take it?

3. Of his three religious inspirations, which one do you think influenced Pope Francis the most? Why?

WRITING PROMPTS

1. Write a letter to Pope Francis. What would you tell him? Would you ask him for something?

2. Choose a chapter and rewrite it as if it were its own story.

3. Imagine that you are a journalist writing an article about a visit that Pope Francis is making to your city. Imagine the places that he would go and the things that he would do.

ABOUT THE ILLUSTRATOR

Ignacio Segesso, from Buenos Aires, holds a degree in the visual arts. As an artist, he has held collective and individual exhibitions at comic conventions as well as in museums and galleries. He was selected in the Hall of Painting at the Quinquela Martin Museum and in the Contemporary Art Week (SAC) in Mar del Plata. He has worked as a colorist for *Patrulla 666*, which received an award at the 3rd Ibero-American Comics Fair. He won the first Proactiva award, which he received at the UNESCO headquarters in Paris. Currently he participates in the *Anthology of Argentine Heroes* and works on his project *Buenos Aires in Vignettes*, which was honored by the Buenos Aires City Government.

READ MORE

Kramer, Barbara. *Pope Francis. National Geographic Readers.* Washington, D.C.: National Geographic, 2015.

Monge, Marilyn, and Jaymie Stuart Wolfe. *Jorge from Argentina: The Story of Pope Francis for Children.* Boston: Pauline Books & Media, 2013.

Woll, Kris. *Pope Francis: Catholic Spiritual Leader. Newsmakers.* Minneapolis, Minn.: Abdo, 2015.

INTERNET SITES

Use Facthound to find Internet sites related to this book.

Visit www.facthound.com

Just type in 9781515791621 and go!

Check out projects, games and lots more at
www.capstonekids.com

INDEX